Old Ninety Six

Old Ninety Six

A History and Guide

Robert M. Dunkerly and Eric K. Williams

from Dunkerly   *Eric K. Williams*
Feb 23, 2009

Charleston   London

History
PRESS

Published by The History Press
Charleston, SC 29403
www.historypress.net

Cover Images: Militia firing line. Volleys of fire were intended to demoralize the opponent. Typical of militia, these men carry a variety of weapons and equipment. This canon is a six-pounder, of which Greene's army had four to use during the siege. It was not enough artillery, in terms of number or size, to batter the defenses.

First published 2006

Manufactured in the United Kingdom

ISBN 1.59629.114.1

Photos courtesy of Ninety Six National Historic Site unless otherwise noted.

Library of Congress CIP data applied for.

Contents

Acknowledgements

The authors wish to thank the following people who helped with this project in one way or another. The staff of The History Press gave us the opportunity to tell this story; we are grateful. Robert's mother, Mary Dunkerly, read the draft and made valuable comments. Karen Smith, ever patient, was willing to play tourist on a hot summer day and walk the trenches. Her input and keen observations were absolutely crucial. Michael Scoggins assisted with locating important sources. John Robertson, who is a talented cartographer, produced the excellent maps. Dr. Bobby Moss answered questions about his research on Loyalist accounts of the battle and unit strengths. Dr. Stan South graciously assisted the authors with visually reconstructing the long-gone structures at Ninety Six and shared his findings from years of digging at the site. The staff of the Abbeville County Public Library provided valuable assistance. Eric's wife, Jan, provided encouragement, insight and valuable suggestions in the course of writing this book. Daughter Rebecca eagerly showed her dad some new computer techniques as he worked on the project.

Introduction

Ninety Six National Historic Site is perhaps one of the richest archaeological sites of the American Revolution in the South. Site of two Revolutionary battles, two Cherokee War battles, a trading post, three forts and two towns, Ninety Six's history spans over three hundred years. This quiet little national park holds the key to our understanding the multilayered history of the Carolina Backcountry. Ninety Six was the center of colonial activity in this region, and the site holds tremendous potential for study and scholarship in the years to come. Its importance to the early history of South Carolina cannot be underestimated. This tour guide uses both historical sources and archaeological information to give visitors a feel for the complex legacy and unique historical and archeological significance of Ninety Six National Historic Site.

There are several theories about how Ninety Six got its name. One story which has prevailed for many years states that in the early 1700s English traders gave it the unusual name because they estimated the location to be ninety-six miles from the Cherokee village of Keowee (to the northwest) in the upper South Carolina foothills. By the mid-1700s, European colonists found it a favorable place to settle.

In 1760, Cherokees twice attacked Fort Ninety Six, which the settlers had built for protection. Located at the crossroads of twelve roads and paths, the village of Ninety Six reached its peak in the 1770s. This important Backcountry town boasted a growing population, twelve houses, taverns, shops, a newly constructed courthouse and a jail.

Ninety Six figured prominently in the Southern Campaign of the American Revolution. The first land battle south of New England was fought here in 1775.

The town changed hands many times during this civil war between Americans who fought for independence and those who remained loyal to England. A second engagement, the longest siege of the entire American Revolution, occurred here in May and June of 1781. By the close of the war, the armies had left the town in ruins. Today the well-preserved Star Fort is a lasting reminder of the tragic lives and times of soldiers and civilians caught up in the intense struggle for the South Carolina Backcountry.

The park is located on Route 248, two miles south of the modern town of Ninety Six, and covers 989.14 acres. A visitor center features a museum with dozens of artifacts and exhibits. A ten-minute video is shown upon request, and books and souvenirs may be purchased here. The one-mile paved walking trail allows visitors to explore historic roadbeds, reconstructed siege works, the original earthen Star Fort, the reconstructed stockade fort and much more. Because of its importance to the founding of our nation, Ninety Six National Historic Site became part of the National Park Service in 1976.

We encourage readers to refer to the endnotes, either on the trail if they have time or at home, because many of them contain additional information that is not included in the main text.

History of Ninety Six

Perhaps no other historic colonial site in the Carolinas is able to give us a window into the past as well as Ninety Six. This little-known town was the center of activity for the region in its day, and the Ninety Six story touches on many important themes of colonial history, including exploration and settlement, Native American relations, the growth of early American society, African American history, the French and Indian War, the American Revolution and many other important topics.

Early inhabitants of the area were living here as early as 9000 BC. In fact, in the summer of 2005 archaeologists found a Clovis point, a projectile point or arrowhead from this early period—an extremely rare find in South Carolina.[1] Over the intervening centuries, the climate and environment of the Southeast changed from mixed forest to closed canopy hardwood forest. Hunter-gatherer bands grew and began concentrating in smaller areas.[2] From 9000 BC through AD 1000 (the Paleo-Indian period through the Mississippian period), hunter-gatherers roamed the woods of the Ninety Six region, evolving into ever more complex social groups and developing decorative ceramics, weaving techniques and more sophisticated agriculture.[3]

The western region of modern South Carolina was home to many Native American groups before the arrival of English settlers in the early 1700s, including the Waterees, Congarees and Saludas. These peoples were largely displaced by other native groups by the time explorers arrived in force. The dominant Native American presence was the Cherokee, and it would be this group that would draw trade from the coast, ultimately leading to the building of the town of Ninety Six.[4]

A scientific study of the area observes that during the pre-settlement era, "this environment is thought to have contained high densities of oak, hickory and white-tailed deer on a seasonal basis. The structure of this resource base provided an opportunity to exploit the…Piedmont in the fall and early winter when acorns and hickory nuts ripened and deer populations aggregated to feed on the nuts. Accordingly, the…model predicts human subsistence-settlement system for the inter-riverine zone involving temporary or seasonal dispersion of human population into small procurement stations, hunting camps."[5]

The Native Americans lived in a world of oaks, hickory, elm, locust, poplar, tulip poplar, walnut and chestnut trees. In the lower, damper areas one found ash, birch, black gum, cedar, dogwood and sweet gum trees. Periodic burning of the land by the American Indians opened areas for farming and provided grazing for animals. Game included turkey, deer, squirrel, rabbit, fox, raccoon, beaver, muskrat, skunk, wildcat, quail, bison, wolves and panthers.[6]

Ninety Six's importance, from its early beginnings to the Revolutionary period, stemmed from its roads. The site was located along the Cherokee Path, which ran from Charleston to the Cherokee towns in western South Carolina, and a road from Ninety Six ran west to the Savannah River.[7] By the 1730s traders, hunters and trappers from Charleston were penetrating this region. Early travelers found an abundance of wildlife and a fertile, inviting territory. Settlements remained relatively close to the coast, and few towns and roads traversed the interior of the state.[8]

The name "Ninety Six" is thought to have come from the estimated distance to Keowee, one of the prominent Cherokee towns (in fact the distance is greater). While there are many other legends and stories related to the origins of the name, historians generally accept this interpretation. References to the name appear in historic records as early as 1737. In fact, George Hunter, the surveyor to the Royal Governor, traveled to the colony's Backcountry and wrote the numerals "96" on his map in 1730.[9]

Ninety Six gained importance in 1746 when Governor James Glen held a conference there with Cherokee leaders. Glen hoped to negotiate the Cherokee's continued friendship with England as war between England and France raged for control of North America. In 1747, the English negotiated to purchase land from the Cherokee in exchange for ammunition. All the land between Long Cane Creek and Ninety Six was now open to settlement.[10]

In 1751, land speculator John Hamilton purchased several thousand acres and had the property surveyed. Incredibly, the old survey line is still visible today and runs diagonally southwest to northeast through the park. Since the 1700s, property owners' lots have bordered the old survey, and as a result one can see old fence lines and cleared areas plainly marking Hamilton's original line.[11]

The early settlers arriving here, including the English, Scotch-Irish, German and French Huguenots, established homesteads and began clearing the land. Large numbers of Africans also lived in the region. Settlers planted crops such as wheat, corn, indigo and flax and their small farms supported cattle, hogs and sheep.[12]

Robert Gouedy, the most famous and influential settler in the area, arrived in 1751. Initially purchasing 250 acres along the Cherokee Path, Gouedy was a trader who intended to establish a permanent post at the site. He imported rum from Charleston for trade with the Cherokee, primarily for deerskins.[13]

Gouedy eventually owned over fifteen hundred acres and raised wheat, tobacco, hemp, corn, indigo and peaches. He owned cattle, sheep and horses. Thirty-four slaves labored on his land as carpenters, wagon drivers,

Commerce with the Cherokee first drew settlers to the region in the early 1700s. Note the various trade goods in demand on the colonial frontier.

coopers and field hands.[14] Gouedy's trading post became a center of activity, a place where travelers could find lodging, send mail, purchase supplies and obtain news. Colonial records indicate that he sold cloth, beads, needles, thread, tools, gunpowder, lead and rum—all the necessities of the frontier. But his activities caused some concern among colonial officials who were apprehensive of his selling rum to the Cherokee.[15]

Gouedy wielded tremendous power in the area. He hunted down one trader who defaulted on his debt, and with the help of two constables and six assistants, confiscated four slaves from the man When he died in 1775, Gouedy had nearly five hundred persons indebted to him. He left property to his wife Mary, son James and daughter Sarah, and left 150 pounds each to his three mixed-blood Cherokee children: Peggy, Kiunague and Nancy.[16]

As more settlers flooded into the area, the quality of life declined for the American Indians, and tensions grew between the English and Cherokee. The Cherokee were involved in a conflict with the Creeks to the west, which added to the tension on the frontier.[17] In the spring of 1751, Ninety Six and other settlements became a haven for refugees driven out by the Cherokee and fleeing from the west.

The growing trouble between Indians and settlers in the Carolinas was part of a larger conflict brewing in North America. Violence broke out in western Pennsylvania in 1754 when a young Virginia militia officer, George Washington, attacked a French patrol. The French and Indian War, or Seven Years' War, raged until 1763, and resulted in France surrendering her North American colonies.

South Carolina responded to the mounting tensions by establishing ranger companies to patrol the frontier, assisted by local Indian scouts. Captains Robert Gibson and James Francis, each with a company, moved across the midsection of the state, hunting down the roving Cherokee. In July 1751, Gibson's troops camped about a mile north of the Ninety Six town site.[18] In 1752, Governor Glen was able to negotiate a tenuous peace treaty and an uneasy calm settled over the region. Another treaty with the Cherokee in 1755 transferred much of central and western modern-day South Carolina to the English.[19]

Tensions with the Indians on the Carolina frontier increased in 1754, as they did elsewhere in Virginia and Pennsylvania. In May 1756, Governor Glen traveled to Ninety Six with military forces. The colonial government began building Fort Loudon in the Cherokee territory to protect settlers, keep the Cherokee loyal to the English and offset French advances from the Gulf Coast. South Carolina troops built and garrisoned the frontier post of Fort Loudon in modern-day eastern Tennessee.[20] In June a large number of cattle arrived at Ninety Six to supply the troops and were driven on to Fort Loudon by soldiers.[21]

Glen was at Ninety Six in early June when he learned of his recall and the appointment of William Henry Lyttleton as the new governor. It had been a trying time for Governor Glen; he had dealt with a boundary dispute with North Carolina (not settled until 1773), Indian raids, negotiations for land with the Cherokee and Catawba, war with France, the arrival of Acadian refugees from Nova Scotia and New Brunswick and a growing colonial population.[22]

Relations with the Cherokee continued to worsen, heightened by the murder of a group of Cherokee hunters near the Edisto River in the winter of 1757–58. To placate the Cherokee, the colony ordered supplies sent from Gouedy's trading post as gifts to the Cherokee leaders. Among these gifts were blankets, trade muskets, axes, rum, lead, knives, powder and cloth.[23] Unfortunately, more Indians were murdered, this time by Virginians collecting a bounty offered by the state for Cherokee scalps. This violence, combined with the aggressive efforts of the French to court Native American alliances, cooled Cherokee relations with the English. Governor Lyttleton had ranger companies patrolling the frontier, and settlers and traders began fleeing east.[24]

In November of 1759, Governor Lyttleton assembled an army and began marching from Charleston, stopping at Ninety Six on the way to the Cherokee towns. In December the English and Cherokee signed a treaty there.[25] By this time, Ninety Six was an important stopping point for English colonial forces traveling to the frontier. The site consisted of Robert Gouedy's house and trading post, a barn and some outbuildings. Governor Lyttleton ordered his troops to scout "for a proper Place to build a Magazine and Stockade-Fort to secure Ammunition and Provision, and a Retreat if necessary: to save Time, Expense and Trouble, Mr. Gouedy's Barn was fixed on for a Store-house, and it was resolved to stockade it in."[26]

Thus, the first fort at Ninety Six was a makeshift fortified barn built in a week's time. The fort consisted of upright logs set into an earthen embankment. Two bastions stood at opposite corners and inside a firing step allowed defenders to fire over the wall. A gate secured access to the fort. Inside, the barn was converted into a storehouse and the men built sheds to serve as temporary barracks. Local militia, civilian volunteers and slaves all worked to complete the fort. While the governor and the bulk of the army went on to the Cherokee towns a small garrison, primarily of sick men, were left at Gouedy's.[27]

Captain Dudgeon described the fort that was built as follows: "This Fort is of the Star kind with four angles, the Exterior side Ninety feet, a simple stockade without a Ditch Erected…to secure a large Convenient Barn ready Built, which was converted into a Store House to Lodge Provissions & in…But from its Construction & Situation has neither the Strength nor advantages Requisite for a Post of Consequence."[28] No drawing was made of this fort since, as Dudgeon wrote, "the Accidentally breaking of my Theodolite the only Instrument I had for the purpose rendered me Incapable of Executing this part of my duty." Such an illustration would have been a valuable guide to archaeologists working on the Gouedy site.[29]

Full-scale conflict broke out in the region on February 1, 1760, when Cherokee warriors attacked a settlement in the nearby Long Canes area. Forty settlers who had been on their way to Augusta to seek refuge were killed or captured. Just two days later, on February 3, the Cherokee struck at Ninety Six, firing at the fort from the cover of the woods. After two hours the attackers left, having lost only two men. The raiders attacked other settlements a few days later. Forty settlers were killed at the fork of the Broad and Saluda Rivers.[30]

This first battle at Ninety Six was a small affair. The garrison knew that the Cherokee were in the area because a patrol had captured two warriors the day before. On the night of February 2, Andrew Williamson's family arrived in Ninety Six, chased by Indians. As they ran in through the gate, a bullet passed through his coat sleeve.[31] To prepare for the assault, Captain James Francis had his men tear down most of the outbuildings to prevent their use as cover in an attack. Forty-five men, including twelve slaves, defended the post on February 3.

A young man known as Young Warrior probably led the Cherokee attackers. The Indians fired from a distance, and their gunfire had little effect, though they did manage to burn Gouedy's house and the remaining outbuildings. Inside the barn one man was grazed on his forehead by a bullet and another was shot through the ear.[32] One settler wrote to Governor Lyttleton that the Indians "have burnt All Gouedy's House Except the little fort you built Round his Barn where he and Capt. Frances [sic] and Some few more are penn'd up."[33]

Throughout the Ninety Six region, families gathered together seeking shelter from the invading Cherokee. Often "forts" were nothing more than private homes with windows boarded up and otherwise modified for defense; the simplest method was placing wooden stockades around the house, as was done at Gouedy's barn.[34]

In the following months supplies continued to flow into Gouedy's trading post. The fort was improved with a well dug inside the stockade, but smallpox broke out among the garrison. Two-thirds of the men were down with the deadly and contagious disease, one of the most feared in colonial America.

Overcrowding, poor diet and bad sanitary conditions often caused such outbreaks in isolated forts.[35]

The Cherokee launched a second assault at Ninety Six on March 3, with over two hundred warriors attacking. For thirty-six consecutive hours the Cherokee fired at the fort from the cover of the woods. Captain Francis again commanded the determined defenders. The Cherokee learned a relief force was coming and withdrew, but not before burning the nearby houses and killing all the cattle within twenty-two miles of the fort. The defenders had several wounded and found six Cherokee dead upon leaving their fort.[36]

The war had turned into a cycle of violence and revenge, bringing each side to adopt crude and bloody tactics. Francis wrote afterward: "We had the Pleasure, During the Engagement to see several of Our Enemy Drop, and We have now the Pleasure…to fattn our Dogs with their Carkases, & to Display their Scalps, neatly Ornamented on the Top of Our Bastions."[37]

Another account of the battle noted that

> about 240 or 250 Indians attacked the Fort…and fired upon it for 36 Hours, without scarce any Intermission, even during the whole Night, but never came within 60 yards of the Stockade, except one Fellow, who was killed and scalped, and whose Body was given to the Dogs, and his Scalp hoisted along-side of the Colours, to provoke the Enemy to come nearer. On Tuesday Morning the 4th, Major Lloyd with 11 men got into the Fort as a Reinforcement, during a hard Shower of Rain, while the Indians were sheltering themselves, and raised the spirit of the Garrison a good deal. In the Fort, one Man was shot thro' the Shoulder, and another in the Mouth; the Ball lodging in the Back of his Neck' but they were both likely to recover.[38]

The raids continued with twenty-five settlers killed on March 10 near the head of Congaree Creek. On April 4, Indians attacked a hunting party sent from the fort in search of turkeys. One man was killed and a boy taken prisoner. The boy later escaped, returning to Gouedy's fort where he told the garrisons that the Indians had eight scalps with them, three of them black and five white.[39]

Eighty wagons of flour arrived at Ninety Six in April, escorted by the Light Infantry of the Twenty-Second Regiment; for the first time British Regulars arrived. An officer with the detachment, Christopher French, wrote: "Here stands a small fort of Picquitts of no consequence, the Country about it as far as clear'd pleasant enough." Another observer with the expedition wrote that there was "a stockade, and a great number of miserable people, chiefly women and children, cooped up in it."[40]

In May, Gouedy's son James was taken prisoner, but Gouedy's influence among Cherokee leaders secured his release after a week. Another important event occurred that same month, when Colonel James Grant and more British troops arrived. They camped, according to French, "about half a mile from the Fort in the Wood." Accompanying the troops were Mohawk, Catawba and Mohican guides (these tribes were friendly to the English).[41]

Colonel James Grant had been involved with another expedition into frontier territory: the 1758 Forbes Campaign in western Pennsylvania that captured Fort Duquesne from the French. Even though Grant had been defeated in a badly managed reconnaissance prior to the fort's capture, he gained valuable experience in frontier warfare and working with the Native Americans. Grant would go on to have a successful military career with the British army in North America. With the Forbes Campaign he also worked with the commander of the Virginia troops, Colonel George Washington.[42]

The Seventy-seventh Highlanders served at Ninety Six during the Cherokee War in the 1760s. These soldiers are demonstrating use of the broadsword.

Over the next few days more troops arrived, bringing the strength to twelve hundred men from the Seventy-seventh Highlanders and First Foot. Local militia joined them. The new troops joined the command of Colonel Archibald Montgomery who intended to bring the war to the Cherokee and end their raids.[43]

The army remained only a few days at Ninety Six, but purchased 337 pounds worth of supplies from Gouedy. On May 18 Montgomery and Grant left for the west. The British army met defeat in eastern Tennessee later that June, leaving the Cherokee issue unresolved.[44] More reinforcements arrived in South Carolina to bolster the war effort. Colonel James Grant assembled 1,300 troops in Charleston for the new mission. The colony raised seven new ranger companies of 75 men each. In April of 1761, 220 men led by Colonel Thomas Middleton arrived at Ninety Six from Charleston, bringing fifty wagons of flour.[45]

Middleton began replacing the stockade around Gouedy's and enlarging it for the other troops to follow. The men tore down one side of the wall and moved it out ten yards to accommodate more supplies. While the new larger fort was sometimes referred to as "Fort Middleton," it was more often called "Fort Ninety Six."[46]

Grant's main force arrived on May 14. Joined by the survivors of Montgomery's army, nearly three thousand troops were stationed at Ninety Six, as many or more than would be present at some Revolutionary War battles like Kings Mountain or Cowpens. Just a few days after the army assembled there, the troops marched west to take on the Cherokee again.[47] Grant's forces entered the Cherokee towns and wreaked havoc, burning crops and destroying villages. They fended off attacks and forced the Cherokee to negotiate a peace treaty in December of 1761.[48]

Back at Ninety Six, on June 20, 1762, the Cherokee brought in several prisoners they had taken. Family and friends met them at Gouedy's fort, and in July the English brought Cherokee prisoners to exchange for them.[49] The close of the war brought peace and prosperity to the settlers of the region.

What happened to the new, larger fort remains unknown. While it may have been maintained for a period, references to it disappear after 1761. By the 1770s, it had clearly been abandoned, or pulled down to salvage materials for other buildings. A new village began to grow just north of the site of Gouedy's fort, along the Island Ford Road (Cherokee Path). A small town took root here and settlers poured into the region. More unrest lay ahead of them, however, though this time not from a foreign threat, but internal strife.[50]

As settlement pushed farther west, away from the capital at Charleston, the need for legal reform urgently grew. The eastern Charleston-based government was unable to effectively manage and support the growing western settlements. Land, for example, was taxed at the same rate across the colony, meaning that property owners in the west paid the high rates for land that had been established in the eastern, more settled areas. There were also fewer services in the interior—no schools, poor roads, few churches and, most importantly, no courthouses.[51]

As Ninety Six was located six days' ride from Charleston, settlers could not conduct legal business, attend a worship service or easily gain access to their leaders in Charleston. The population of the entire Backcountry (including the Camden, New Acquisition and Ninety Six Districts) has been estimated at about thirty thousand, of which probably ten thousand were African American. This far outnumbered the population of the Lowcountry around Charleston.[52]

Other problems arose in the Backcountry. Without courts or legal supervision, settlers squatted on land claimed by others. Bandits robbed travelers and stole cattle and horses. Counterfeiting was rampant. Murders went unsolved. Help was too far away in Charleston, and local settlers organized the Regulator movement to restore order in the Backcountry.[53]

In the fall of 1767 local leaders met and agreed "to execute the Laws against all Villains and Harbourers of Villains." Perhaps four thousand Regulators organized and began patrolling the roads and enforcing laws in the Backcountry from the Pee Dee region to the Ninety Six District. They hunted criminals and subjected offenders to whipping and flogging.[54]

Ninety Six was the center of the movement in the area between the Broad and Savannah Rivers. Resident James Mayson became their leader and helped organize the Regulators in the area. Rather than rebelling against government control, the Regulators wanted more control and petitioned Charleston for approval of their actions.[55]

In September of 1768, a body of men met at Ninety Six to discuss traveling to Charleston to vote and elect representatives who were favorable to their views. By the next year the colonial government responded to the crisis in the Backcountry and the Regulator movement lost steam. Its lasting impact, however, was to make the upcoming Revolutionary War bloodier and more bitter, as groups took revenge for earlier atrocities in the Backcountry.[56]

There was another important effect of the Regulator movement. In 1769, the Colonial Assembly finally addressed the necessity of Backcountry courts. The assembly divided the colony's interior into seven judicial districts and authorized the construction of courthouses and jails in each. These were semi-annual courts, and circuit judges rotated through the districts of the Backcountry to oversee the sessions. The Ninety Six District was a huge tract of land that included all of present

Edgefield, Saluda, McCormick, Abbeville, Greenwood, Newberry, Laurens, Union and Spartanburg Counties, as well as part of Aiken and Cherokee Counties.[57]

By November of 1772, the same year as the Gaspee Incident and the formation of the Committees of Correspondence in New England, workers completed the courthouse and brick jail in Ninety Six. While Americans in Rhode Island and Massachusetts were beginning to question English authority and were establishing the means to communicate with each other, settlers in the Carolina Backcountry were building a frontier town. The large, imposing structures of the jail and courthouse gave this frontier town a semblance of permanence and ensured its importance to area residents.[58]

The court's first session was held on November 16, 1772. Robert Stark served as the first sheriff, and James Pritchard the first clerk of court. Sessions at Ninety Six were held in April and November, and court days were important gatherings in the small town. Cases included horse stealing and counterfeiting, common crimes in colonial America. Colonial justice was administered to three convicted horse thieves in Ninety Six, with each receiving thirty-nine lashes and having his right ear cut off.[59]

The town played an important role as tensions grew with England and the Revolution broke out. The first battle south of New England occurred here in 1775, illustrating the divided loyalties of the area residents. In June of 1775, news reached South Carolina of the fighting that had occurred on April 19 at Lexington and Concord, Massachusetts. In Charleston a provisional congress met to form an independent government. On September 15, Royal Governor Arthur Campbell fled to a British warship in the Charleston Harbor, leaving the colony in the hands of the Americans.[60]

To secure the support of the Backcountry, the provisional assembly sent William Henry Drayton and Reverend William Tennent into the western regions to bolster enthusiasm for the war effort and contain Loyalist activity. They also hoped to seek assurances that the Indians would not join the British in the coming struggle. Drayton set up headquarters at Ninety Six in September and assembled over two hundred militia. He sent out a circular stating he intended to "explain to the people at large the nature of the unhappy disputes between Great Britain and the American Colonies…to quiet their minds, to enforce the necessity of a general union." No easy task in an area threatened by Indian raids, possessing few roads and towns and divided by years of violence and upheaval.[61]

Drayton wrote that he fortified the buildings at Ninety Six as best he could and sent patrols of militia out to scout for the Loyalists. He observed that "the courthouse was not musket proof and the prison could not contain a third of our men. I fortified the prison by mounting a gun in each room below, in each of which I placed a small guard; I lodged the powder in the dungeon." With the existing buildings unable to accommodate the garrison, work began on a makeshift fort nearby.[62]

In the meantime, forces loyal to England were organizing in the Backcountry, watching with apprehension as Drayton and Tennent gathered their troops. Loyalist forces seized a shipment of gunpowder sent by the provisional congress to the Cherokee as a sign of friendship. Militia commander Major Andrew Williamson gathered his troops and assembled them at Ninety Six to meet this Loyalist threat after Drayton and Tennent had moved on.[63]

Loyalists Captain Patrick Cunningham and Major Joseph Robinson had gathered about 1,900 men to attack Ninety Six. Major Williamson, with about 562 men, had a crude fort hastily constructed on high ground behind the jail, incorporating the barn and outbuildings of John Savage's plantation. Williamson abandoned the jail and town, concentrating his men at the fort. The garrison had only four beef cattle and thirty-eight barrels of flour for provisions.[64]

Cunningham's forces arrived on November 19, 1775, and demanded Williamson's surrender, which he refused. For a full day both sides watched and

James Mayson was an important figure during the early settlement of the Ninety Six region, and fought in the first battle in 1775. Seen here is his grave.

observed the other. Two of Williamson's men left the fort, attempting to get to Spring Branch, and were seized by the Loyalists. Both sides now opened fire. Inside the tiny fort, the defenders dug a well forty feet deep "through a very tenacious clay soil" to gain access to water.[65]

The Loyalists never stormed the fort, but fired at it from the cover of outbuildings and other shelter. Loyalist troops also used the two-story brick jail to fire on the fort. The next day Cunningham's men tried to burn the defenders out, igniting the field and fences near the fort. Using this as a smokescreen, a force of Loyalists under Major John Robins advanced using a mantelet (wooden shelter) of sticks and branches to approach the fort and set it on fire. The mantelet accidentally caught fire and the plan was abandoned.[66]

Major James Mayson wrote of the siege:

> We had, at most, not more than five hundred men. At first consultation with Major Williamson, we agreed to march and meet the opposite party and give them battle; but, upon consideration, we thought it most prudent to march all our men to Col. Savage's old field, near Ninety-Six, as our numbers were small, compared with the other party, and to fortify the same place with the rails thereabouts. We arrive there about day break, and in about two hours a square of one hundred

Militia firing line. Volleys of fire were intended to demoralize the opponent. Typical of militia, these men carry a variety of weapons and equipment.

This small field piece is typical of those used on the colonial frontier. It required a coordinated team to fire the gun.

and eighty-five yards, was fortified in such manner as to keep off the enemy; but before three days had expired, our men began to be outrageous for want of bread and water, and we had not above sixteen pounds of gunpowder left. On Tuesday last, in the afternoon, the enemy held out a flag of truce and sent into our fort a messenger with a letter from Major Robinson to myself.[67]

The firing lasted for three full days until a truce was arranged. On the evening of November 21, a Loyalist waved a white flag from the jail and asked to negotiate. Meeting by candlelight, they agreed on a cease-fire. Williamson's force was allowed to march out, destroy Fort Ninety Six, fill in the well and hand over their swivel guns (small artillery pieces). The Loyalists would not attack them in their withdrawal and would return the guns three days later.[68]

This was the first Revolutionary War battle at Ninety Six, and it was a rather bloodless affair. The rebels under Williamson had one killed and twelve wounded; James Birmingham was the sole fatality. Cunningham's forces lost Captain Luper and had fifty-two wounded.[69]

The town would remain in American hands until the arrival of British forces in 1780. After retaking the post, the British fortified the strategically important frontier town. Back under royal control, it served as a staging area for Loyalist and British expeditions. Major Patrick Ferguson assembled his army here before marching into western North Carolina and later, defeat at Kings Mountain.

The following year, Ninety Six became even more important to the British as American forces entered the state and began attacking strong points. On the evening of May 21, 1781, Major General Nathaniel Greene and his force of a thousand American troops arrived at the British outpost. From May 22 to June 18, Greene's forces staged the longest siege of the Revolutionary War against about a thousand Loyalist and British troops who were defending Ninety Six. Many of the area's Loyalist refugees crowded into the village for protection. Devastated by years of conflict, Ninety Six never fully recovered. The site was soon abandoned and the town of Cambridge grew up nearby.[70]

Founded in 1787, Cambridge sat on the high ground east of the old town, where the Black Swan Tavern and Route 248 now sit. The town took its name from the college founded there, one of the three institutions authorized by the state in 1785. Little more than an academy, Cambridge College included a brick building along modern-day Route 248, and a few log structures. Reverend John Springer served as the first rector.[71]

The early town boasted a post office, seven stores, a brick church in the center of town and about ten or fifteen houses. James Wilson, the first postmaster, was appointed by George Washington.[72]

One citizen left his description of how the Revolution was remembered in antebellum America. He related the festivities for July 4, 1806:

> *A very fine morning. We began the celebration of Independence in the Carolina way, this morning, by participating in a flowing bowl of Egg-Knogg…About 11 o'clock three companies of cavalry, artillery and infantry were arranged and exercised by Brigade Major Butler…The dinner was in a little thicket not far from the village and consisted chiefly of roast beef and pork cooked over fires that were kindled in a long trench dug in the ground, about a foot deep. About 200 dined together. The tables were served by negro slaves under the superintend of the mangers.*

By the end of the day people were "eating, others talking and laughing and others sauntering about." James Gouedy, son of early settler Robert Gouedy and a local celebrity, was present at the celebration.[73]

By the 1820s the town had over ten stores, four hotels, a courthouse, library and post office. Lots were laid out along the main street, Broadway. Several things caused its decline by mid-century. The college, never large, closed in 1825. A flu

James Gouedy was the son of the first settler at Ninety Six, Robert Gouedy, who operated the trading post that stood here in the 1750s and 1760s.

epidemic swept the area, and the railroad went to nearby Greenwood. By the 1850s the brick buildings had been dismantled and many families left.[74] At least one store remained until 1840, and the post office existed until 1860. Nevertheless, Cambridge slowly faded, and today nothing of the town remains above ground.

Ninety Six was the center of attention again just a handful of times. In 1878 a large crowd gathered at the site to commemorate the battles fought there. The event included a review of the local militia by Governor Wade Hampton, military bands, speeches by dignitaries and other festivities. In the 1960s, interest in preserving the site increased during the bicentennial of the American Revolution.[75]

The following tour guide goes into more detail of the Revolutionary events of 1781 that occurred at Ninety Six.

Battlefield Tour

This tour follows the park's guided walking path and takes about an hour and a half. Begin by walking the path from the visitor center into the woods. As you leave the visitor center, note the small swivel gun to your right at the end of the wooden walkway. According to members of the local Star Fort Chapter of the Daughters of the American Revolution the gun was found on the grounds of nearby Roselands Plantation.

Stop 1: Spring Branch

From the visitor center proceed down the path and stop at the first marker, titled "Spring Branch."

The Spring Branch was the primary water source for the colonial town of Ninety Six and later for the occupying British forces. During the siege in the hot weather of May and June water was scarce for the king's troops and civilian refugees alike. General Greene's American soldiers realized the importance of this spring to the British and posted guards to watch it. Archaeologists theorize that the water was clearer and flowed more freely in the 1700s.

Stop 2: Island Ford Road

Proceed to the marker titled "Island Ford Road."

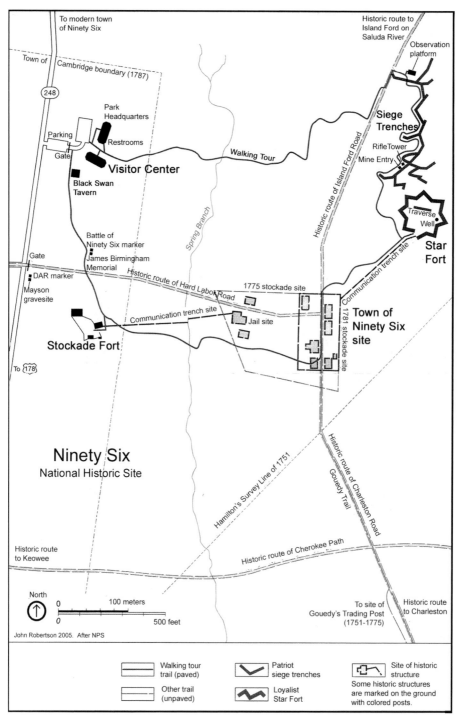

This map shows the walking tour route and important features. *Map by John Robertson.*

Below you is the Island Ford Road, one of the major roads running through the town of Ninety Six. Keep in mind that the landscape has changed greatly. While today you see areas of green fields and woods, in 1781 the area surrounding the town would have been cleared for firewood, construction and an open field of fire (removing any potential cover for attackers near the fort and town). Crops and pastures stood around the town, where now a second growth forest stands. All around you, where trees now stand, were open fields in 1781.

Lieutenant Anthony Allaire, a Loyalist officer serving here, wrote that "Ninety Six is situated on an eminence, the land cleared for a mile around it, in a flourishing part of the country, supplied with very good water, enjoys a free, open air, and is esteemed a healthy place." Another Loyalist, Dr. Uzal Johnson of the New Jersey Volunteers, wrote of the scenery that "Natural growth is Oaks, Black Walnut, Hickery, etc., which are very large and thrifty." Around the town he observed fields of "wheat, Indian corn, oats, Hemp, Flax, Cotton and Indigo."[76]

This photo shows the variety of uniforms and equipment found among Greene's army during the 1781 siege.

Loyalist troops in 1781. The defending garrison consisted of a mix of Loyalist provincials in red coats, along with local Loyalist militia.

Stop 3: Observation Tower

Move ahead and pause at the second marker in the roadbed. Ascend the tower for an excellent view of the 1781 siege lines.

Below you are the reconstructed American siege lines, excavated and rebuilt in the 1970s. Keep in mind that only the location of the trenches was found at the time; they were not fully excavated, so what you see does not represent their true depth.

Here you get a perspective that no American soldier ever had: a bird's-eye view of the Loyalist defenses. The Star Fort anchored the Loyalist defense and Greene immediately made it his primary objective. Colonel Kosciuszko advised concentrating on the Star Fort, the strongest part of the enemy's defenses, because once that was weakened, the rest would easily fall. In the distance to the right, hidden by the modern trees, was the town and stockade fort. Greene observed that the defenses were very strong, writing: "Our success is very doubtful."[77]

The primary defensive position at Ninety Six was the Star Fort. This was the focal point of Greene's 1781 siege. These trenches are original, among some of the best-preserved Revolutionary War earthworks in the nation.

The siege got off to a rocky start on May 22, 1781, when American forces began work on a battery and trench fortification just seventy yards from the British fort, about where the second parallel (trench) currently is. It was much too close to the Star Fort and during the night of May 23, a Loyalist raiding party under Lieutenant John Roney of DeLancy's Brigade attacked, driving off the Americans and capturing several slaves and many of their tools. Greene was furious and ordered great care taken with entrenching tools from then on.[78]

During the night of May 28, the Americans started over on the first parallel, set farther back from the Star Fort, where you now stand. While some men dug, others stood guard facing the British lines. Troops completed the first parallel on June 1. From here the soldiers dug zig-zag trenches, known as "saps," to move closer and establish a second parallel. Often the work was, as Captain Robert Kirkwood described, done "under a Scattering Fire from the Enemy all night." Somewhere behind you, about a mile away, was the American camp, though its exact location has not yet been determined.[79]

Stop 4: Artillery Position

The next stop is located at the six-pound cannon. As you move ahead the tour stops only at certain markers. Pause as you go to read all the markers you pass for a fuller understanding of the siege.

Here the Americans positioned an artillery battery. Imagine the exhausted men dragging the guns through the trenches, crouching down while under fire, and manhandling the guns into position. The artillery emplacement was an earthen fortification about twenty feet high with wooden platforms for the guns. The cannons needed the wooden support beneath them since the recoil of firing would eventually tear up the earth below. Building the artillery emplacement up so high in this clay, under constant enemy fire, would have been backbreaking work. General Nathaniel Greene wrote: "We are pushing on our approaches, but for want of more fatigue Men the Work goes on slow."[80]

Siege warfare called for batteries to be placed at intervals along the approach lines. As the besiegers were able to move the artillery closer, their ability to batter the defenders increased. Moving from the first to the second and finally the third parallel was the standard procedure for siege operations. Here at Ninety Six the hard clay merely absorbed the cannonballs; artillery fire did little damage to the Star Fort. For more information on siege warfare, see appendix B.

The gun before you is a replica six-pounder (artillery was classified by the size of its shot). Greene's army was fortunate enough to have four of these six-pounders (which were the largest field guns used by armies at the time) but the Americans still did not have enough artillery to support the siege.

These are the reconstructed trenches that the Americans gradually dug toward the Star Fort. *Photo by Karen A. Smith.*

NINETY SIX MYSTERY: The siege was barely underway a week when five supply wagons arrived from Augusta on May 30, 1781. Upon examining the cargo one of General Greene's officers discovered two small African American sisters who were eight and six years old. When asked, none of the wagoners had any knowledge of them. The next day the officer interrogated the girls. They said that their master's name was Johnston and that the wagoners had taken them away. When asked where they lived, neither could remember. Nothing else is known about these two young girls, but their fleeting presence echoes the tragic stories of so many.[81]

Stop 5: Second Parallel

Move ahead to the marker labeled "The Second Parallel."

By June 3, Americans had completed the second parallel here. Amid the neat grassy mounds it is difficult to remember that once, open muddy trenches stretched across the ground in front of you. Digging trenches in the hard clay under a June sun was backbreaking, fatiguing work, especially while being fired upon by the Loyalists in the Star Fort. General Greene wrote that "not a man could shew his head but what he was immediately shot down." A private soldier, William Vaughn from Virginia, recalled that his company was "fighting the enemy, for fifteen days and nights, with but little interruption."[82]

The zig-zag sap trenches allowed the besiegers to approach without being directly fired on by the defenders. The Americans established a rotation so that each regiment did time in the trenches and then got to rest back at the camp. While in camp, soldiers performed routine duties like maintaining weaponry and personal gear, stockpiling supplies, filling sandbags, gathering sticks for fascines and weaving gabions. Fascines were large bundles of sticks and branches about six feet long. They were placed horizontally on the trench walls with wooden stakes driven through them to add strength and stability to the walls. Gabions (large bottomless wicker baskets placed upright and filled with earth) supported the walls of the trenches and served as material for building up artillery emplacements.

As the work progressed, Cruger's Loyalist defenders launched nightly raids to disrupt the work. Several from both sides were killed and wounded in these fierce night battles.

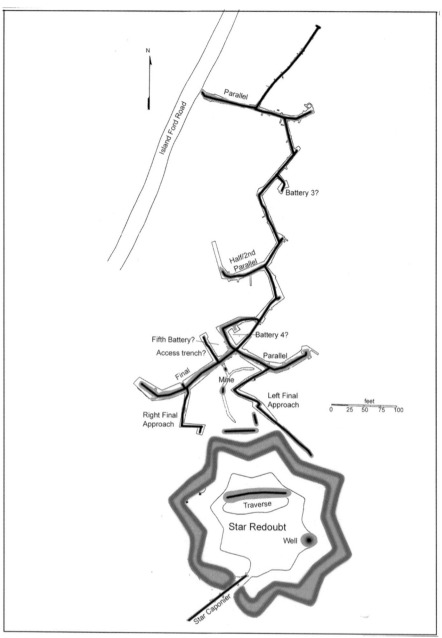

This map shows the Americans' trenches facing the Star Fort. Archaeologists located these trenches in the 1970s. The dark areas are the original trenches; the outlines are the areas exposed by the archaeologists. *Map by John Robertson.*

A Point to Ponder: If General Greene had had a mortar…
A mortar was an artillery piece with a short, stubby, thick barrel. It fired an exploding projectile in a high arc over a fort. Field guns, like the six-pounders Greene had, fired directly at a target and were not well suited to sieges. Since the Americans didn't have any mortars, we can only speculate that the siege may have had a much different result!

Stop 6: The Rifle Tower and Mine

Proceed to the marker for "The Rifle Tower." Visitors are reminded that for their own safety, climbing the tower or exploring the mine is prohibited.

The Americans tried everything to break the Star Fort, including the classic siege tactics of bombardment, cutting off water supplies, and even constructing a tower and a mine. But a dogged and determined defense by the Loyalists prevented them from ever breaching the walls. By June 10 the third parallel, in front of the tower, was complete, and the Americans were just yards from the Star Fort. As you gaze at the Star Fort, bear in mind that the walls were originally ten to twelve feet high, steep, and had an intimidating ring of abatis (felled trees with sharpened branches facing the enemy and other deterrents) around it.

This reconstructed rifle tower is only one-third the height of the original structure. From here American marksmen tried to fire into the Star Fort. *Photo by Karen A. Smith.*

On the night of June 13, the Americans built a thirty-foot-high tower that enabled them to fire down into the fort. Greene posted riflemen (some of the best shots in his army) in the tower. Cruger's men responded by raising their walls six feet higher with sandbags. The defenders also tried to batter the tower down with red-hot cannon shot from the Star Fort, but the wood was too green and would not catch fire. The present reconstruction is only ten feet high, so you must imagine a tower three times as tall standing here.[83]

Greene tried to maintain military discipline, especially in the siege lines. He wrote that individuals "not having particular business" be kept "from entering into the Trenches, or crowding the Batteries; as great confusion may arise from the gratification of an idle Curiosity."[84]

Now move ahead to the marker for the mine.

Kosciuszko also had the Americans attempt to blast the Star Fort from below with a mine, another classic siege tactic. Begun on June 9, a shaft was dug down

Taken from inside the Star Fort, this shows the Loyalist defenders' perspective of the American lines. In the distance the rifle tower and battery positions are visible. *Photo by Karen A. Smith.*

and then divided into two tunnels. The attackers planned to pack the main tunnel with explosives, detonate them and charge through the resulting gap in the massive earthen wall of the fort.

The mine was an underground tunnel 3½ feet wide and 3½ feet tall. It was 125 feet long from end to end. Its outline is marked on the ground with rope. Digging was excruciatingly slow, and the siege ended before the mine could be completed. The clay soil is so hard that the mine still exists with well-preserved shovel and pick marks visible in its earthen walls! The mine at Ninety Six is a completely unique feature from the Revolutionary War because it is still open underground—no better example of eighteenth-century military tunneling exists in the nation today.[85]

The Americans also tried firing flaming "African" arrows from their muskets to set fire to the wooden roofs of the town's buildings. Bound with flax string and treated with pine pitch, they were lit and fired out of muskets into the town (to the right beyond the fort). Cruger simply had his men remove the wooden shingles from the town's buildings—with each attempt the Americans made, Cruger's men rose to the occasion to counter them.[86]

This mine, dug by the Americans to blast through the Star Fort, was not finished before the siege ended. *Photo by Karen A. Smith.*

This view inside the mine was taken in 2003 during archaeological excavations; the mine still exists under the ground. Here, Americans dug over one hundred feet by candlelight in the rock-hard soil.

A Point to Ponder: One evening while Colonel Kosciuszko was inspecting the mine, a night raiding party from the Star Fort suddenly appeared. As Kosciuszko attempted to get away he was wounded in the buttocks by a Loyalist bayonet. The London press made the humorous, satirical comment saying that he had been "wounded in the seat of honor."[87]

Stop 7: The Attack

Continue along the trail to the marker labeled "The Attack" and face the Star Fort.

Realizing that the mine was progressing too slowly and British reinforcements were coming to aid the attack, General Greene decided to give up the siege. His officers and men, however, urged one last effort to capture the fort. Convinced, Greene organized an attack on the Star Fort and stockade fort. Regimental commanders made a "Minute Inspection" of arms and ammunition and were told to "return what is bad." Each soldier was issued thirty good rounds of ammunition, some of which were buck and ball cartridges (a large musket ball and three small shot), giving each man greater killing power.[88]

Before you lies some of the most hotly contested ground of the Revolution. From near where you now stand the American forlorn hope moved out to assault the fort on June 18. Of the fifty who crawled out of the trenches, one half were killed or wounded.[89]

Greene timed the assault on the Star Fort for noon, preceded by an artillery bombardment. Led by Lieutenants Samuel Selden of Virginia and Isaac Duval of Maryland, Continental troops and militia scrambled out of their earthworks. Some were armed with axes to cut through the fort's outer defenses and some had long wooden poles with hooks to pull down the defenders' sandbags. A group of determined pioneers went first, hacking their way through the abatis that ringed the fort. Abatis consisted of felled trees with sharpened branches facing the enemy. Bear in mind that the fort's dry moat was about five feet deep, with steep banks to discourage easy access. Protruding from the walls were fraises (sharpened wooden stakes) that prevented anyone from climbing the slope.[90]

This canon is a six-pounder, of which Greene's army had four to use during the siege. It was not enough artillery, in terms of number or size, to batter the defenses.

Under the sweltering summer sun, these ragged and dirty Continentals charged out through a hail of gunfire. In response, Major Joseph Green of DeLancey's Brigade sent out a party of Loyalists who circled around the far side of the fort and stopped them in their tracks in hand-to-hand combat. Between fire from the fort and the counterattack, Greene's final effort failed. He wrote afterward, "The behaviour of the Troops on this occasion deserves the highest commendations, both the Officers that entered the Ditch were wounded, and the greater part of their Men were either killed or wounded. I have only to lament that such brave Men fell in an unsuccessful attempt."[91]

A POINT TO PONDER: While Lieutenant Samuel Selden of the First Virginia was charging the fort's steep wall trying to pull off sandbags, he was wounded by a musket ball. A later account of the incident described "a [musket] ball entering his wrist, shattering the bone of the limb nearly to his shoulder." For severe wounds such as this the only remedy was amputation. The surgeon usually had assistants to hold down the patient and the limb. "To this end Selden would not submit. It was his right arm he was about to lose. He sustained it with his left [holding his right hand with his left] during the operation, his eyes fixed steadily upon it, nor uttered a word, till the saw reached the marrow, when in a composed tone and manner he said, 'I pray you Doctor, be quick.'"[92]

A NOTE OF INTEREST: On your right, in the field is a small, unmarked cemetery discovered by archaeologists in 1974. It contained only three graves, two adults and a child. Although the identities of those buried are unknown, archaeologists theorize that the graves date to about 1810 and were probably area residents.[93]

Stop 8: The Star Fort

Proceed along the trail to the fort and stand in the entryway.

The Star Fort used an unusual and ingenious design that permitted enfilade fire, which allowed defenders to catch attackers in a crossfire, no matter what direction they came from. Few attacks ever succeeded in the face of enfilade fire. The Star Fort's walls are original, and are an example of some of the best-preserved Revolutionary War earthworks in the nation. There were more famous sieges, yet few original earthworks remain from Yorktown, Charleston, Savannah or elsewhere. The walls of the fort originally stood fourteen feet high, and the ditch and wall were steep to prevent good footing (erosion has since worn them down). In front of the moat would have been the abatis to slow down attackers as they approached.[94]

To your right, inside the fort, note the depression of the well that the Loyalists dug. After twenty-five feet they failed to find water, so the well was abandoned and slaves brought in water at night. In front of you stands the traverse, a fallback defensive position in case the Americans breached the wall. It also provided protection from the riflemen atop the nearby tower.[95]

During the assault on June 18, Provincials under Major Green garrisoned the Star Fort. The Provincials were Americans who had enlisted into the British military. Issued the traditional scarlet coats and military equipment, they were well trained and were the equivalent of British Regulars. When the Americans assaulted the fort, Lieutenant John Roney and Captain James French led a party out and around the far side of the fort to flank them, and the counterattack stopped their progress. Roney paid with his life.[96]

Enter the fort and move ahead to the wall opposite the American rifle tower.

Peer over the walls to see the defenders' perspective of the American trenches. Be careful not to walk on the fragile earthworks. Here you can see how the rifle tower, three times as high as what you see today, threatened the safety of the Star Fort's defenders. As you walk through this fort, imagine the desperation of the garrison in this tiny space, under constant infantry and artillery fire.

As you leave the fort, note the markers on your left for the communications trench, known as a caponier ditch. Archaeology showed this connecting trench to be $3\frac{1}{2}$ feet deep and 3 to 5 feet wide at the top, sloping to 2 feet wide at the bottom. Back and forth, crouched over for protection, couriers relayed messages, slaves ran supplies and troops moved to and from the town, taking their turn in the Star Fort.[97]

NINETY SIX MYSTERY: During the siege local civilians visited the American camp to sell goods to the soldiers. A local legend speaks of a woman named Kate Fowler who regularly visited Greene's camp selling food and other articles. One day she drove her wagon through the camp and up to the trenches, where the American guards failed to stop her. She spurred her horses forward, making a break for the fort. The Loyalist guards let her in, and Kate delivered a message to Cruger: reinforcements were coming. For the first time the garrison knew that Lord Francis Rawdon, with British Regulars and Loyalist militia, were marching to their aid. Who was Kate Fowler and did she really deliver the message? We will probably never know.[98]

Stop 9: The Town of Ninety Six

Continue along the walk to the marker for "The Town of Ninety Six."

You now stand in the midst of colonial Ninety Six, once the center of activity for the South Carolina Backcountry. Its importance stemmed from the convergence here of many roads. The barrenness of the site today belies its significance. Robert Gouedy first settled near here in 1751, establishing a trading post. Following the Cherokee War of 1760 the settlement grew into a town, with a blacksmith, mills, jail and courthouse. Loyalist officer Anthony Allaire wrote that about a dozen buildings stood here in 1781.

It is difficult for modern visitors to imagine the importance of Ninety Six to its colonial residents. Business and trade flourished here, and government buildings like the jail and courthouse (primitive as they may seem to us) provided contact with the outside world and brought justice, law and order to the Backcountry. As

Many local families sought refuge in the town during the 1781 siege.

Women in the garrison would have performed important services like treating the wounded and baking food.

you walk through the town site on the old Charleston Road, imagine buildings lining the streets and residents going about their business.[99]

From here Major Patrick Ferguson left with his Loyalist militia on a mission to conquer the Backcountry, which ended in defeat at Kings Mountain. During his brief tenure here Ferguson recommended a series of improvements of the town's defenses. From the summer of 1780 to August of 1781, Ninety Six was a Loyalist stronghold, where refugees and families could seek shelter from bands of attacking Americans.

Ninety Six was fortified in 1776 with a palisade wall (upright logs) that included the jail (ahead on the tour) inside its perimeter. This stockade included an area just over four acres. During the first battle, in 1775, Loyalists had attacked an American force in the stockade fort. The town no doubt suffered during this first battle as structures were damaged and residents fled for safety. In 1781 the palisade was moved in to cover a smaller area that Cruger felt would be easier to defend. British officer Major James Wemyss wrote that the fortified town was "about one hundred yards square, with Block House Flankers." The defenses were so strong that British engineer Lieutenant Henry Haldane wrote they were "in a much better state than [he] expected."[100]

When Greene's army approached the town in May 1781, Cruger set his men to improving the defenses even more. One observer described this frenzied activity: "Its houses, which were intirely [*sic*] of wood, were comprised within a stockade. The commandant immediately set the garrison both officers and men, to work to throw up a bank, parapet high, around this stockade, and to strengthen it with an abatis."[101]

The garrison troops camped with their equipment in the area enclosed by the palisade wall. Remember that many local Loyalist families, refugees in the face of Greene's advancing army, had crowded into the fort, further putting a burden on supplies and water for Cruger's garrison.[102]

Among the civilian refugees were people like Moses Myer (an express rider), John Murphy (a carpenter) and Jane and Arthur Henderson, an elderly couple nearly seventy years old who sought shelter in the fortified town. As overcrowding increased, disease became a major concern for the garrison. Cruger had anyone who came down with smallpox, like Jacob Odom, removed from the fort to outlying areas.[103]

In 2005 archaeologists placed trenches here to find the site of the town's southern defensive wall. These four parallel trenches found the faint remains of that wall. This view looks across the field past the Gouedy Trail. *Photo by Robert M. Dunkerly.*

In the summer of 2005 archaeologists returned to Ninety Six and conducted testing along the town's defensive walls. They located the defensive walls on the eastern and northern edge of the town. The ditch and well were located, and the moat was found to be about ten feet wide. Very few artifacts were located, but some early nineteenth-century pottery fragments indicated that the ditch was filled in soon after the siege, as records indicate.

A NOTE OF INTEREST: The sunken trace of the Whitehall Road is to your right. By the 1770s the road extended about fifteen miles west to Whitehall Plantation, owned by local cattleman Andrew Williamson.

This trench exposed the edge of the ditch that surrounded the town's 1781 wall. The darker soil on the right-hand side indicates fill in the ditch, the lighter soil on the left is the historic ground level. Archaeologists use the different colored soil to locate features. *Photo by Robert M. Dunkerly.*

This view looks across the ditch. The moat was about ten feet wide, and the removed earth was piled up to support the upright wooden stakes that formed the town wall. *Photo by Robert M. Dunkerly.*

This trench shows the depth of the defensive ditch. The soil colors are visible on the right side of the trench wall. The lighter soil slopes downward, showing the profile of the ditch. *Photo by Robert M. Dunkerly.*

These early nineteenth-century ceramics were discovered in the southeast corner of the town's defensive ditch. These artifacts, by their date, tell us when the ditch was filled in. After the town was abandoned and Cambridge was founded, the ditch may have been used for a trash depository. *Photo by Robert M. Dunkerly.*

NINETY SIX MYSTERY: During an excavation, archaeologists discovered an artifact of particular interest: a conch-type seashell. Who brought the shell from the seacoast and why? Perhaps a child or a settler picked it up as a souvenir of their long journey to the South Carolina Backcountry. Or it could have been left behind by one of the many Africans who lived in Ninety Six, as shells were highly valued by Africans in the colonial period.[104]

At this point if your time permits, you may take the optional tour of the Gouedy trading post area. This will add an additional hour to your visit. See Page 61 if you wish to take this additional tour.

Stop 10: The Jail

Move farther down the path to the jail.

Ahead of you is the jail site; its remains are buried today. The sturdy jail was an important part of the town's defenses. A brick jail in the Backcountry was a symbol of power and permanence at a time when most residents lived in one-room wooden homes with dirt floors. It was thirty-four by forty feet and had three stories, which gave defenders a tall, commanding position during the siege. In the jail archaeologists have found a 1775 English halfpenny, nails, kettles for cooking, earthenware pots and jars, cattle and pig bones (proof of what was cooked and eaten here). They also found gun parts like flints, ramrod pipes, trigger guards, hammers, lock plates and brass side plates—all from British muskets. Modeled after the Charleston jail, the Ninety Six Goal (pronounced "jail") fell into disrepair after the Revolutionary War. Later residents may have taken the bricks (made by slaves) for reuse in houses or outbuildings. Archaeologists discovered that much of the walls had caved in, covering the cellar.[105]

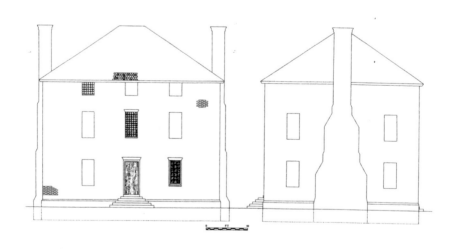

Architectural reconstruction, front and side elevations

This is an artist's sketch of what the jail may have looked like, based on archaeological evidence and historical accounts. The two-story jail, which stood here during both the 1775 and 1781 sieges, was the most imposing structure in the town. *From Jerome Green's* Historic Resource Study.

Built in 1772, in response to the violence and upheaval of the Regulator period, the jail symbolized stability and law and order on the frontier. In the early 1760s, violence and instability on the frontier forced many to take justice into their own hands. As many as four thousand "Regulators" formed vigilante groups to deal with outlaws and Indian attacks. Completion of the jail and courthouse at Ninety Six helped calm the frontier and brought a measure of justice and stability to the region. Some of the Loyalists defending the town had actually served time in this jail when Ninety Six was held by the Americans.[106]

Loyalist troops converted the jail into a stronghold during the 1781 siege. Loyalist officer Alexander Chesney wrote that "I was sent to garrison the goal of Ninety Six Which I fortified."[107]

As you walk to the next stop, note the deep valley and stream. Because the siege took place in one of the hottest months, water was critical to the Loyalist soldiers and refugees. Slaves from the garrison, stripped naked, were sent by the Loyalists down to the creek through the communications trench at night for water. Many other blacks, some free, some runaway slaves, served with the garrison as soldiers. The South Carolina militia kept a constant watch on the stream, firing on soldiers who approached from the town.[108]

Stop 11: Stockade Fort

Make your way up the trail to the entrance of the stockade fort. Note the markers for the communication trench's location to your right. Through this trench slaves gathered water for the garrison and troops moved back and forth between the town and stockade fort.

The current reconstruction shows the stockade fort of 1781, which guarded the water supply and western approaches to the town. One of the log buildings has a finished roof with wood shingles. The other building outlines represent the locations of log structures that archaeologists discovered. Earlier, Andrew Williamson's fort of 1775 also occupied this site and the first battle of Ninety Six was fought here. Accounts state that Williamson's fort was flimsy, made of beef hides and hay bales, but archaeologists found it to be well built after locating traces of its earthen defenses.[109]

The stockade fort included a ditch eight to ten feet wide inside the stockade wall, with an inner firing step for defenders on the inside, and posts that were three to five feet in diameter. The firing step allowed defenders to load while under cover then step up to fire over the wall. Archaeologists found the charred remains of the posts in the ground, along with indications of the fort's earthen walls. Artifacts found here include buckles, musket balls (.69 caliber,

The stockade fort. Both the site of Williamson's 1775 fort and the 1781 stockade fort, this site saw action in both battles.

for French muskets), a shilling, a bone button, green glass fragments from storage bottles, rib bones from pig and cattle and slipware and creamware (types of pottery).[110]

Walk in and explore the fort. At the swivel gun post in the corner, look out across the fields toward the modern road. There, in the distance, were the Americans' trenches.

Most of the activity during the 1781 siege occurred on the plain facing the Star Fort, until June 7, when Colonel Henry Lee's Continental troops arrived after capturing the British fort at Augusta, Georgia. The arrival of these troops, with news of the success at Augusta, boosted the morale of Greene's army. Lee's forces (his own Legion and the Delaware Regiment) began laying siege to the stockade fort from the west, the area beyond the modern road ahead of you, in the distance. Archaeologists have found that their trenches approached within thirty-seven yards of the stockade fort, and were over two feet wide and three feet deep. Lee's artillery soon began pounding the fort.[111]

On June 12, Lee tried to take the fort by sending a chosen party to storm it. Sergeant Whaling and twelve privates snuck up and began setting fire to the abatis surrounding the fort. They were discovered by the guards and in the

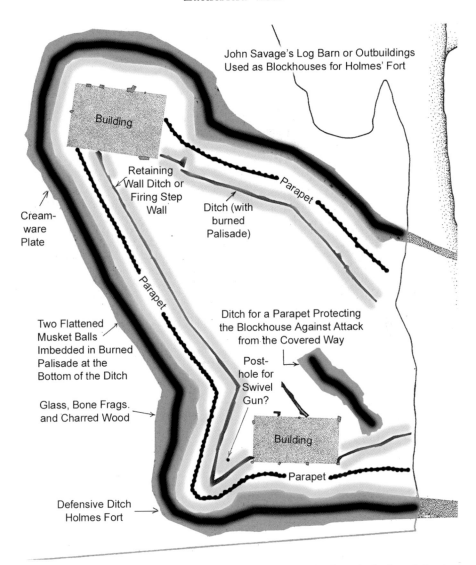

This map shows archaeological features at the stockade fort, including defensive ditches and walls, post holes for buildings and military and domestic artifacts. *Map by John Robertson.*

firefight Whaling and five other men were killed and five wounded; only one man of the twelve escaped injury. Private Edward Sims recalled that he was badly wounded in the left ankle and "lame ever since."[112]

As part of the grand assault on June 18, Lee's troops surged forward to attack the stockade fort while Campbell's men attacked the Star Fort. Lee captured the stockade fort in about an hour, and from here his men were able to fire onto the town's western wall, located across the valley (where you came from). With news that the attack against the Star Fort had failed, Lee withdrew to his original positions.[113]

After leaving the stockade fort, pause by the James Birmingham Memorial to your right. Birmingham was an American soldier killed in the 1775 battle of Ninety Six that was fought on this site and the first American casualty of the Revolution in the South.

General Nathaniel Greene was the American commander at Ninety Six. *Courtesy of Ninety Six Chamber of Commerce.*

Lieutenant Colonel John H. Cruger, Loyalist defender at Ninety Six. *Courtesy of Ninety Six Chamber of Commerce.*

Lieutenant Colonel Harry Lee commanded American cavalry during the siege. He is the father of Robert E. Lee. *Courtesy of Ninety Six Chamber of Commerce.*

General Andrew Pickens was a talented American militia leader from South Carolina. *Courtesy of Ninety Six Chamber of Commerce.*

Colonel Thaddeus Kosciuszko, Greene's trusted engineer who oversaw the siege operations. *Courtesy of Ninety Six Chamber of Commerce.*

Black Swan Tavern. This historic home dates to 1787 and was moved to the park in 1968. It is now a setting for living history programs.

Stop 12: The Black Swan Tavern and Cambridge

Continue along the path and pause at the Black Swan Tavern.

Now known as the Black Swan Tavern, this well-preserved log house (ca. 1787) was originally built by settler Andrew Logan in nearby Greenwood and was moved to the park in 1968. In the eighteenth century a tavern was more than a place to get a drink. In colonial towns, including Ninety Six, taverns were actually places of business. Here one could receive and send mail, conduct business or have a meeting, get a meal and receive the latest news from abroad. Taverns also served travelers, offering space for sleeping and quarters for horses. Customers rented space in a bed, not an entire room unless they could afford it, so travelers often shared beds or floorspace with total strangers.

You are also now on the site of Cambridge, a town founded in 1787 after Ninety Six had faded. The town's lots were laid out and a few structures were built, including a courthouse. A flu epidemic in 1815 devastated the town, and a few years later the railroad went through nearby Greenwood; soon after the town declined and was eventually abandoned.[114]

Aftermath

The moment General Greene saw the ragged survivors of the assault crawl back into their trenches he knew that the siege was over. His forces were simply not strong enough to take the Star Fort, and with news that Lord Francis Rawdon was on the way with British reinforcements, he knew he had to pull out before they arrived.

General Greene blamed the strong fortifications of the enemy, and his own lack of men, supplies and artillery, for the failure. It was not for lack of trying. Greene wrote to the Continental Congress, "Our Poor Fellows are worn out with fatigue, being constantly on duty every other Day and sometimes every Day. The [enemy's] Works are strong and extensive."[115]

Total casualties for the Americans amounted to 154: 58 killed, 76 wounded and 20 missing. Cruger's forces lost 85: 27 killed and 58 wounded. It had not been a particularly bloody engagement overall, yet Greene's army lost a significant percentage given the numbers engaged. The forlorn hope (the chosen attack force that went first) that assaulted the Star Fort lost about half their numbers. Captain Joseph Pickens, brother of General Andrew Pickens, was killed early in the siege.[116]

Losses, by unit, for the American army are as follows:[117]

	Killed	Wounded	Missing	Total
Headquarters and staff	-	1	-	1
Virginia Brigade	41	36	16	93
Maryland Brigade	13	26	3	42
Delaware Regiment	1	9	1	11
Legion Infantry	2	2	-	4
Virginia Militia	1	2	-	3
Total	58	76	20	154

Cruger sent a note to Greene asking for a prisoner exchange, to which Greene agreed. They established the trade of a regular for a regular and a militia soldier for a militiaman. Greene also asked the Loyalist officer for permission for his men to retrieve and bury the dead that lay in front of Cruger's earthworks. Cruger refused, not wanting the Americans to get too close to his defenses and inspect them. He said the American dead lying within his lines would be sent out.[118]

On June 19 General Greene issued marching orders for the next day. At five o'clock on the morning of June 20, his army broke camp and moved out, marching six miles to the Saluda River by seven. It was none too soon; the British reinforcements under Lord Francis Rawdon arrived the very next day. Rawdon realized the post was too far from Charleston and too deep in hostile territory. The British and Loyalists abandoned Ninety Six by early July, burning the town to deny it to the Americans. Refugees and runaway slaves accompanied the army on its march to Charleston. Many soldiers were lost to sunstroke during their retreat. The two sides had struggled for nearly a month at Ninety Six, with neither side possessing the town in the end.[119]

The following is a passage by local historian Merle McGee of Greenville, South Carolina. His interest in the Southern Revolutionary War battlefields continues to inspire those who work in and visit these special places. Mr. McGee passed away in January 2005. His memorable words are displayed at the park visitor center:

Living Ghosts

There are those who can still hear the drums, bugle calls, marching feet, groans of the wounded, and cannon fire of over 200 years ago. Not everyone hears these sounds and it is a shame that the ones that do are in the minority… They—and only they—realize…just how huge a debt we all owe to the past. Just ask the men who were never buried at Camden or at Hanging Rock…or the bloody Patriots defeated at Ninety Six. May we never forget the prison ship dead floating in the mud of Charleston Harbor. All of their sounds are still out there to be heard if we are still interested enough to listen.

Optional Tour
Gouedy's Trading Post

From the town site, proceed down the trail into the woods. This optional tour of the Gouedy trading post site will take an additional hour. This add-on tour leaves from the town site (Tour Stop 9).

The Gouedy Trail is a loop approximately 1½ miles in length. It was designed to immerse visitors in the natural environment and to make accessible one of the most archaeologically significant and least known areas of the park. Archaeology done by Dr. Stanley South in the early 1970s revealed several significant sites. You can explore them by following the trail down the old Charleston Road. Follow the signs through the field and into the woods. From there follow the blue paint blazes on the trees.

If you decide to walk this informative trail take a brochure from the box at the Gouedy Trail sign. It will be your guide as you view sites from the park's earliest days, including the sunken remains of the original Cherokee Path, the site of Hamilton's survey line, the suspected site of Fort Ninety Six (ca. 1759), a house cellar (ca. 1790s), the grave of Robert Gouedy's son (Major James Gouedy) and the "Unidentified Cemetery," containing about fifty graves of unknown persons. James Gouedy died in 1816 at age fifty, a well-respected member of the community. A Masonic emblem is on his gravestone.[120]

Shortly after leaving the town site the trail will make a bend to the left; at this point you are crossing Hamilton's 1751 survey line, an important landmark in the early settlement of the area. Soon after, you will cross the Cherokee Path, one of the many trading routes that made Ninety Six important. A short while later the trail will break off from the Charleston Road and enter the woods to the right, near the site of Gouedy's trading post.

Old Ninety Six

Here the Cherokee launched two attacks against Gouedy's fortified barn. This remote site was a major supply depot on the trade road from Charleston to the Cherokee villages. Thousands of soldiers, Indians, settlers, traders and slaves passed through here.

Gouedy's flourishing trade included cloth, beads, needles, tools, gunpowder, lead, rum and other necessities. In 1759 the militia built a ninety-foot square stockade around his barn for protection. Known as Fort Ninety Six, this fortification was the one attacked by Cherokees in February and March of 1760.

At the site you will see a depression in the ground; this is a brick-lined cellar that archaeologists explored in 1996. Once thought to be part of the trading post, archaeology has shown that this is a nineteenth-century foundation. Down the trail to your right are about fifty graves. Many are marked by body-length depressions and simple unmarked head and footstones. While this area is thought to be the site of Gouedy's trading post and the first Fort Ninety Six, the locations of the structures have yet to be found.

If you have time, walking the Gouedy Trail is a must. You will get a true appreciation for the rural scenery that Ninety Six's first settlers experienced.

Appendix A
The Armies in 1775

American Militia
Major Andrew Williamson

Numbers in parentheses indicate strength of the units.

Captain James Mayson (37)
George Reed (25)
Andrew Pickens (40)
Aaron Smith (17)
Benjamin Tutt (34)
Andrew Hamilton (23)
Thomas Langdon (12)
Adam C. Jones (26)
Matthew Beraud (13)
Charles Williams (11)
Francis Logan (18)
Alexander Noble (4)
John Anderson (11)
James Williams (28)
Robert McCreery (30)
John Rodgers (20)
Jacob Colson (18)
Hugh Middleton (3)
Francis Singuefield (17)

James McCall (54)
David Hunter (19)
John Erwin (26)
Robert Anderson (18)
Nathaniel Abney (23)
William Wilson (16)
Artillery—Joseph Hamilton (17)

American Army totals: 560 men, 4 swivel guns[121]

These officers each commanded companies of militia at the siege. Many served in other battles and went on to important commands during the war.

Loyalist Forces
Major Joseph Robinson

Captain Patrick Cunningham
Captain Bowman

Loyalist Army total: 1,900 men

The makeup and organization of Cunningham's forces not known. They were, however, all militia from the Ninety Six region.[122]

Appendix B
The Armies in 1781

American Southern Army
General Nathaniel Greene

Numbers in parentheses indicate strength of the units.

Maryland Brigade—Colonel Otho H. Williams (427)
  1st Maryland Regiment—Colonel John E. Howard
  2nd Maryland Regiment—Major Henry Hardman

Virginia Brigade—Brigadier General Isaac Huger (421)
  1st Virginia Regiment—Lieutenant Colonel Richard Campbell
  2nd Virginia Regiment—Colonel Samuel Hawes

Delaware Regiment—Captain Robert Kirkwood (60)

North Carolina Troops (66)

South Carolina Militia—Brigadier General Andrew Pickens (400)

Virginia Militia—Captain Jeremiah Pate (100)

Lee's Legion—Lieutenant Colonel Henry Lee (150)

American Army totals: 1,624 men, 4 six-pound guns

Greene's southern army included a little over 900 Continental troops from Delaware, Maryland and Virginia, and a number of North Carolina troops. Later, troops under Lee and Pickens joined the army midway through the siege.[123]

Veterans of some of the harshest fighting of the war, Greene's core of Maryland and Delaware Continentals were seasoned veterans who had fought in many of the Northern battles around New York City and had endured hardships at Camden, Cowpens, Guilford Courthouse and Hobkirk's Hill.

The Southern Campaign had been hard on these men: the Maryland Line went from seven regiments to two after Camden, and the Delaware Regiment was reduced from eight companies to two after the Camden disaster. Reformed and joined by new Maryland recruits, Greene considered these regiments the backbone of his army.

Joining these experienced troops were the two newly raised Virginia regiments that had fought their first battle at Guilford Courthouse. North Carolina was in the process of raising new Continental Regiments, and they would join Greene later that summer. All of the Continental troops from Virginia and the Carolinas had surrendered at Charleston in May of 1780, and these states were in the process of rebuilding their troops.

Garrison of Ninety Six
Lieutenant Colonel John H. Cruger

Numbers in parentheses indicate strength of the units. (Based on the studies of Dr. Moss.)[124]

Spartan Militia—Major Zacharias Gibbs (120)
Stevens Creek Militia—Captain John Cotton (241)
Long Cane Militia—Colonel Richard King (123)
Little River Militia—Major Patrick Cunningham (224)
Dutch Fork Militia—Captain Daniel Clary (60)
Fair Forest Militia—Captain Shadrack Lantry (88)
3rd Battalion, New Jersey Volunteers—Lieutenant Colonel Isaac Allen (253)
DeLancey's Battalion—Major Joseph Green (165)

Loyalist Army totals: 1,274 men, 3 three-pound guns

Cruger's command consisted entirely of Loyalists; as was common in the South, this battle was fought entirely between Americans. Other than the two Provincial forces, all the defending Loyalists would have been in civilian clothing, nearly identical to Greene's American militia.

The garrison included parts of six Loyalist Militia Regiments raised in the Ninety Six District, as well as the New Jersey Volunteers and DeLancey's Brigade. Many of these Loyalist officers, like Allen of New Jersey, had seen their fair share of combat and were up to the task at Ninety Six.[125]

Many of the Loyalist militia had previously fought for the Americans and then switched sides. Almost three hundred had been with Ferguson at Kings Mountain; they had escaped after their capture and made their way back to the safety of Ninety Six in time to rejoin their units and participate in the siege. One third of the Loyalist militia here had escaped from captivity after Kings Mountain. After harsh treatment and a risky journey south, they no doubt had a score to settle with Greene's army.[126]

While many sources indicate that the Loyalist garrison had only 550 men, more recent research by Dr. Bobby Moss shows that there were well over 1,200 men present at Ninety Six Dr. Moss has extensively researched Loyalist and British military and pension records in the United States, Canada and Great Britain. Jerome Greene, who thus far has produced the only other detailed research on the siege, notes that Cruger had at least 700 men under his command, and probably more.

Appendix C
Siege Warfare

Ninety Six was the longest siege of the American Revolution. For twenty-eight straight days, men dug, scraped and died in the trenches. Day and night, rain or shine, they worked relentlessly in the mud and dirt while under fire. The work was backbreaking and tedious. Red mud stained clothing, stuck to shoes and got into everything the men handled—their weapons, their bedding, their food.

Eighteenth-century sieges included a mix of engineering and etiquette. First, an army approached and surrounded the target, cutting off communication and establishing a secure base. Greene's army approached from the north, surrounded the town and set up a camp somewhere above the Star Fort. Pickets surrounded the roads leading into town to intercept messengers and reinforcements.[127]

Custom demanded that the besieger make a formal request to the garrison first. Greene broke this tradition, however, by immediately digging earthworks much too close to the fort. Cruger responded by sending out a raiding party that disrupted the work and stole the Americans' tools. Chastised, Greene then fell back to properly begin a siege with a first parallel.[128]

Once an attacker had established a first strong trench, or parallel, he could then move forward to prepare a second parallel closer to the enemy. These trenches are called "parallels" because they face the enemy's earthworks; by running parallel to the fort, a first parallel allows the attacker to establish a secure line from which all subsequent siege work will extend.

Besiegers move closer by digging saps (zig-zag trenches that do not directly approach the fort) to avoid direct fire. Saps are angled so that the enemy cannot fire down the length of the trench on the unprotected soldiers. These connecting trenches move supplies, communications and reinforcements back and forth. From the second parallel the attacker can begin placing artillery batteries to bombard and weaken the garrison.[129]

Once the second parallel is complete, the attacker may begin the third. Closest to the enemy, the third parallel will allow the attacker's guns to fire point-blank at the defender and batter them into submission. Greene's forces did not have time to finish their third parallel before it was decided to make a desperate attack. Throughout the month-long siege, Greene constantly requested more men and supplies. He wrote that he did not have enough men or material to effectively besiege the garrison.[130]

Cruger, as was expected, made nightly sorties against the advancing American trenches to interrupt their progress. As was customary, Greene made a formal plea for Cruger's surrender once the Americans were at the third parallel. But Cruger's situation was far from desperate; despite being cut off from outside supply and having trouble getting fresh water, Cruger's defenses were intact, and he knew Rawdon's column was on the way to relieve him. The call for surrender was turned down, forcing Greene to either break off the siege or storm his works.

American officers, with little formal training in siege warfare, were greatly assisted by Europeans like Colonel Thaddeus Kosciuszko here at Ninety Six, or General Rochambeau at Yorktown. Laying out the trenches to the correct alignment, digging to the proper depth, placing artillery for maximum effect and ensuring supplies and materials were properly brought up consumed the efforts of Greene, Kosciuszko and their staffs. As a Polish military engineer, Kosciuszko had been recruited along with several French military engineers by the Continental Congress in 1776. These engineers assisted the newly formed Continental army. Kosciuszko's considerable education and experience provided invaluable assistance in the Americans' siege. General Greene realized Kosciuszko's expertise and delegated to him the primary responsibility for conducting the siege.

Other sieges during the Revolution, like Yorktown, Charleston and Savannah, followed this pattern. When a garrison surrendered, the established rules dictated the next actions. If the attackers felt the defenders had fought admirably, they were allowed to march out with colors flying—the honors of war. There were other important customs. After the British army surrendered at Yorktown, for example, French, British and American officers took turns hosting dinners for their counterparts in each army. While strange to us today, social stature and etiquette pervaded in the eighteenth century, even during war.

Appendix D
Archaeology

Looking at Ninety Six today reveals the value of archaeology; there is little left above ground to tell us what occurred here. Remove the markers, trails, monuments and reconstructed buildings, and we see very few original features. Archaeology has allowed us to see the past as it was and sheds light on the events and people of Ninety Six.

Archaeology is the study of the past through material culture, through artifacts. It is not about "stuff," but about the people who made and used those objects. Archaeologists reconstruct the past by examining the material evidence of what is left behind. The value of archaeology is that it often tells us more than the written record.

Artifacts from a battlefield, for example, can tell us what types of weapons and ammunition were used based on shells, balls and gun parts found. Examining where we find dropped balls and fired balls tells us where troops were firing from and what their maximum ranges were. From other equipment we learn about how an army was supplied and what types of material they used. Food remains tell us about diet and health. The location of artifacts across a site place troop positions and identify campsites, cemeteries, earthworks, etc.

Archaeology rests on the basic principle of stratigraphy, the study of layers in the soil that are deposited over time. The farther down we dig, the farther back in time we are going. Any artifact found in a certain layer dates that layer. Thus, an artifact, like a coin, that we can definitely date, would date all the materials found with that coin.

Features such as defensive ditches, trenches, postholes and foundations of structures appear as different colored soil, as shown in the earlier photographs.

Appendix D: Archaeology

The archaeologist must note the different texture, color and composition of the soil. Finding postholes allows one to play a connect-the-dots of sorts; an arrangement of postholes may indicate a building, each corner having a post. The remains of the rotten post leave a dark round stain that we see in the ground. Other changes in the soil such as charcoal and brick fragments are important clues to past activities.

The archaeology done at Ninety Six in the 1960s and '70s laid the groundwork for our understanding of this site. Archaeologists unearthed the defensive walls that surrounded the town, and uncovered the foundations of buildings. Walls and structures were evidenced by posthole remains: the location of former posts—either palisade posts or building posts.

The first archaeology at Ninety Six occurred in the early 1960s by Dr. William Edwards of the University of South Carolina. Stanley South conducted perhaps the most extensive digs in 1970–71 at Ninety Six village, the stockade fort, Kosciuszko's mine and Fort Ninety Six (ca.1759). Archaeologists also investigated the stockade fort site and the American approach trenches at the Star Fort. Just prior to the site's turnover to the National Park Service archaeologists Michael Rodeffer and Stephanie Holschlag explored several sites including the siegeworks, jail and communication trenches.

From the 1980s to the present several National Park Service archaeological teams conducted a series of smaller exploratory excavations. In 2005 Stanley South returned to Ninety Six for the first time in thirty-four years to conduct exploratory excavations near the old Ninety Six village. The 2005 fieldwork located the defensive ditch and wall that surrounded the town, along with a few late eighteenth-century and early nineteenth-century artifacts. In the future archaeology will remain an extremely important aspect of park management.

Appendix E
The Park Today

Ninety Six National Historic Site preserves the site of the town, battlefields and settlement outposts of this important colonial site. Throughout the year the park offers special events to commemorate the events and honor those who fell in the battles.

After the decline of Ninety Six and Cambridge, the Star Fort remained a popular local landmark. During the 1920s, as part of a nationwide survey of battlefields, the Star Fort was analyzed by War Department historians but not felt significant enough to be preserved as a park (as was done with Kings Mountain), or a monument (like at Cowpens).[131]

In the 1960s the State of South Carolina took an interest in the site and formed a commission to acquire land and develop it as a historic site. Much of the interest was fueled by the upcoming bicentennial. The site was administered by Greenwood County, yet proponents of further protection hoped for national recognition. In 1976 Congress agreed to create Ninety Six National Historic Site, placing it under the care of the National Park Service.[132]

Several monuments stand in the park, and they are listed here.

DAUGHTERS OF THE AMERICAN REVOLUTION MONUMENT
Made of granite, this marker is located alongside SC Highway 248 in front of the park. This monument was brought to the site on the back of a horse-drawn wagon from Greenwood and erected in 1925 by the local Star Fort Chapter of the Daughters of the American Revolution (DAR). It commemorates the site's early settlement and its role in the Revolutionary War.

Just behind the marker are two graves with marble headstones. James Mayson and his wife Henrietta rest here. Mayson was a prominent area settler; he was a soldier during the Cherokee War and a leader of local Regulators. He was later instrumental in persuading the royal government to bring law and order to the Ninety Six Backcountry. Mayson served in the Revolution and remained a prominent leader long afterward.[133]

A bronze marker commemorates the removal of the Maysons' remains in 1939 from the site of Mayson's Glasgow Plantation near the Saluda River to this site.

National Register of Historic Places Marker

This marker is located adjacent to the parking area near the kiosk. It specifies and commemorates Ninety Six's importance as an area of settlement and its role as a focal point of conflict during the American Revolution. It was originally placed on the nearby log house but was placed on this brick base in 1984.

Daughters of the American Revolution Swivel Gun Marker

This unusual marker was moved to its present location in 1983. The local Star Fort Chapter DAR had the iron swivel gun (found a few miles outside the park) mounted on the granite stone in 1953. It had originally been located in Greenwood at the American Legion Building.

James Birmingham Memorial

Located near the entrance to the stockade fort this granite stone is surrounded by an iron fence. The stone was erected to honor James Birmingham, the first South Carolinian to lose his life in the cause for freedom during the American Revolution. He was a member of the Long Cane Militia and suffered a fatal wound from a Loyalist musket ball. During one of archaeologist Stan South's early excavations in the 1970s, skeletal remains in a shallow grave were uncovered within the outlines of Williamson's Fort of 1775. The remains were photographed and removed to the Department of Archaeology and Anthropology at the University of South Carolina for further examination. Are the remains those of Birmingham? The mystery will remain until conclusive evidence proves his identification beyond a doubt.

Appendix F
Ninety Six Timeline

11000 BC	Nomadic hunter/gatherer groups move into the area.
1000–1700	The Cherokee become the dominant Native American group in the region.
1737	The term "Ninety Six" first appears in historic records.
1746	Governor John Glen holds a conference with Cherokee leaders at Ninety Six.
1751	John Hamilton runs his survey line though the area. Robert Gouedy arrives and builds a trading post.
1752	Local militia camps at Ninety Six as ranger companies patrol the frontier
1756	Governor Glen is at Ninety Six when he is recalled to Charleston to be replaced.
1759	Governor William Henry Lyttleton stops at Ninety Six at the head of an army on the way to meet the Cherokee. Gouedy's barn is fortified, the first fort at Ninety Six is built.

1760	Ninety Six is attacked twice by Cherokee. Montgomery arrives at Ninety Six with British Regulars on their way to fight the Cherokee.
1761	Thomas Middleton arrives to expand the fort; Grant's army of three thousand men follows. Fort is soon abandoned; the town grows north of Gouedy's trading post.
1762	Prisoner exchange between English and Cherokee at Ninety Six as the war ends.
1767	Regulators organize at Ninety Six.
1768	Regulators meet at Ninety Six and plan to march on Charleston.
1769	A courthouse is authorized for Ninety Six; Regulator crisis winds down.
1772	Courthouse and jail completed; first court session held at Ninety Six.
1775	William Henry Drayton arrives at Ninety Six on his Backcountry mission, organizing local militia to counter the Loyalists. First Revolutionary War battle of Ninety Six; Loyalist and Americans fight a three-day battle and end with a truce.
1780	British forces from Charleston capture Ninety Six and begin expanding its fortifications. Major Patrick Ferguson assembles his army here then marches toward the Carolina frontier and Kings Mountain. Survivors of the Kings Mountain defeat drift back to Ninety Six.

1781	British improve defenses; they build the Star Fort and construct a smaller, stronger stockade around the town. General Nathaniel Greene's army besieges the fort for twenty-eight days (longest siege of the Revolution). Lord Rawdon's British forces liberate the town, yet soon abandon it and destroy the fortifications.
1787	Town of Cambridge grows near Ninety Six.
1815	Flu epidemic strikes Cambridge.
1855	Cambridge is all but abandoned.
1878	Celebration held at Star Fort to mark ninety-seventh anniversary of the siege; about four thousand attend.
1920s	War Department examines Ninety Six and other Revolutionary War battlefields; does not recommend preservation at this time.
1960s	Greenwood County creates a historic site at Ninety Six. First archaeological excavations begin.
1970s	Extensive archaeology at Ninety Six.
1976	Ninety Six becomes a National Park Site with Congressional authorization.
2000	225th anniversary of the 1775 battle is commemorated.
2004	Archaeologists map and photograph the mine.
2006	225th anniversary of the 1781 battle is commemorated.

Notes

1. Guy Prentice, *Archaeological Excavations Conducted at Ninety Six National Historic Site*, (Tallahassee, FL: Southeast Archaeological Center, 2002), 24.

2. Ibid., 25.

3. Stephanie Holschlag, Michael Rodeffer and Mary Cann, *Greenwood County: An Archaeological Survey*, (Greenwood, SC: Lander College, 1979), 7.

4. Jerome Greene, *Historic Resource Study and Historic Structure Report, Ninety Six: A Historical Narrative* (Denver: National Park Service, 1978), 1–2.

5. Prentice, *Archaeological Excavations*, 23. Rather than entering a region untouched by man, the European explorers and settlers of the 1700s found an area that had been very much manipulated by the Indians. Periodic burning had opened fields, hunting had depleted certain species and abandoned villages were visible reminders of the previous occupants.

6. Holschlag, Rodeffer and Cann, *Greenwood County*, 5.

7. Greene, *Historic Resource Study*, 3. These roads made Ninety Six a gateway for settlement once Europeans arrived in large numbers. Throughout its history, Ninety Six would be important because of its location in the local road network.

8. Ibid., 5.

9. Ibid., 4, 6.

10. Ibid., 7; Prentice, *Archaeological Excavations*, 47.

11. Greene, *Historic Resource Study*, 7. The Hamilton Survey Line is most easily seen in aerial photos, where vegetation and field patterns clearly show that the line has been used for over two hundred years to mark property boundaries.

12. Thomas H. Pope, *The History of Newberry County*, (Columbia: University of South Carolina Press, 1973), 5. These crops were the staples of diet and furnished the materials needed for textile production among settlers.

13. Greene, *Historic Resource Study*, 10.

14. Ibid., 10, 55.

15. Ibid., 10, 19.

16. William McDowell, *The Colonial Records of South Carolina: Documents Relating to Indian Affairs*, (Columbia: South Carolina Archives Department, 1958), 42–47; Margaret Watson, *Greenwood County Sketches*, (Greenwood, SC: Attic Press Inc., 1970), 13.

17. Greene *Historic Resource Study*, 13; McDowell, *Colonial Records*, 17–18.

18. McDowell, *Colonial Records*, 32, 42. In fact, many important leaders who would be involved with the Revolution in South Carolina fought in the French and Indian War in Pennsylvania and Virginia. Edward Lacey and Daniel Morgan are examples.

19. Greene, *Historic Resource Study*, 16, 17; Pope, *Newberry County*, 2.

20. Greene, *Historic Resource Study*, 20.

21. Ibid., 20–21.

22. Stitt W. Robinson, *James Glen*, (Westport, CT: Greenwood Press, 1966), 103, 118. In fact, the border between the Carolinas remained an issue through the 1700s and into the 1800s, resulting in a controversy over where future president Andrew Jackson was born. (To this day he is still claimed by both states.) The border was still being re-surveyed in the mountainous western regions as late as 2001 and 2002. The Acadian refugees were French settlers of modern Nova Scotia who were forcibly removed when the English captured the territory. By dispersing the French civilians the English hoped to strengthen their hold on this newly won territory.

23. Greene, *Historic Resource Study*, 22.

24. *South Carolina Gazette*, December 8, 1759; McDowell, *Colonial Records*, 456–7.

25. Greene, *Historic Resource Study*, 23.

26. *South Carolina Gazette*, December 8, 1759.

27. Ibid.

28. Greene, *Historic Resource Study*, 25.

29. Ibid. A theodolite is a surveying instrument used for making measurements. They were used to produce maps as well as lay out angles and points in construction.

30. Ibid., 28; Richard M. Brown, *The South Carolina Regulators*, (Cambridge, MA: Belknap Press, 1963), 9.

31. Greene, *Historic Resource Study*, 30.

32. Ibid., 31.

33. McDowell, *Colonial Record*, 495–6.

34. Greene, *Historic Resource Study*, 29.

35. Ibid., 31–32.

36. Ibid., 32.

37. Ibid.

38. *South Carolina Gazette*, March 15, 1760.

39. Greene, *Historic Resource Study*, 34; Brown, *South Carolina Regulators*, 7.

40. Greene, *Historic Resource Study*, 35, 36.

41. Ibid., 34, 36.

42. Paul Nelson, *General James Grant*, (Gainesville: University of Florida Press, 1993), 32. Washington gained valuable combat experience on the Pennsylvania and Virginia frontier, and met many future officers of the later Revolutionary War, both English and American.

43. *South Carolina Gazette*, April 7, 1760.

44. Greene, *Historic Resource Study*, 36–37.

45. Ibid., 38; Pope, *Newberry County*, 23.

46. Greene, *Historic Resource Study*, 38–39.

47. Ibid., 39.

48. Ibid.

49. Ibid., 40.

50. Ibid., 43.

51. Brown, *South Carolina Regulators*, 139; Pope, *Newberry County*, 77, 86.

52. Greene, *Historic Resource Study*, 46; Brown, *South Carolina Regulators*, 18. South Carolina's Regulator movement differed from the one in North Carolina in important ways. Settlers in the Southern province wanted more, not less, government control, and were more willing to work with the authorities in Charleston. North Carolina's Regulators were reacting to administrative corruption and inefficient management. Theirs was a true rebellion against the authority of the Royal Governor, while South Carolina's Regulator movement hoped to bring stability, not political change.

53. Brown, *South Carolina Regulators*, 17–18.

54. Greene, *Historic Resource Study*, 48; Brown, *South Carolina Regulators*, 113.

55. Greene, *Historic Resource Study*, 48. The Regulator movement was an important but often overlooked aspect of South Carolina colonial history, being overshadowed by the coming of the Revolution. The Regulator violence left many scores unsettled among the frontier settlers, and made the later Revolutionary War more divisive and brutal than it may have otherwise been.

56. Ibid., 49.

57. Pope, *Newberry County*, 32.

58. Greene, *Historic Resource Study*, 51; Robert M. Dunkerly, *More Than Roman Valor*, (Baltimore: PublishAmerica, 2003), 38. The Gasepee Incident was a major event on the road to war between the colonies and England. Smuggling was rampant in New England, as merchants tried to avoid duties and taxes. British warships routinely inspected ships and patrolled the coast to enforce royal maritime laws. One such warship, the *Gaspee*, ran aground in Rhode Island after chasing a smuggler. Local citizens burned the ship, and the event stiffened resolves on both sides of the Atlantic.

59. Greene, *Historic Resource Study*, 54; Pope, *Newberry County*, 32.

60. Prentice, *Archaeological Excavations*, 56; Dunkerly, *Roman Valor*, 51. As with North Carolina

and Virginia, the Royal Governor of the colony fled to an English warship and attempted to retake the colony. Loyalists were unable to rally in sufficient numbers and English intervention failed at Fort Moultire in June of 1776, leaving the state in the hands of the Americans until the British arrived in force in 1780. The long period of American control, in which Loyalists were persecuted, exiled and harassed, left bitter resentment and contributed to the later violence that broke out among the population in 1780 and 1781.

61. Prentice, *Archaeological Excavations*, 56; R.W. Gibbes, *Documentary History of the American Revolution*, Vol. 1, (Spartanburg, SC: Reprint Co., 1972), 163. The importance and long-term ramifications of this expedition have often been overlooked by historians.

62. Gibbes, *Documentary History*, 174.

63. Prentice, *Archaeological Excavations*, 56.

64. Ibid.; Gibbes, *Documentary History*, 217.

65. Prentice, *Archaeological Excavations*, 56; Greene, *Historic Resource Study*, 70.

66. Greene, *Historic Resource Study*, 70.

67. Gibbes, *Documentary History*, 70.

68. Ibid., 218; Prentice, *Archaeological Excavations*, 56–57.

69. Gibbes, *Documentary History*, 219.

70. Watson, *Greenwood County Sketches*, 32.

71. Ibid., 22, 5.

72. Ibid.

73. Ibid., 26. This provides an interesting view of patriotic celebrations in antebellum America.

74. Ibid., 27, 32.

75. Ibid., 31, 2; Hugh Wilson and W.C. Bennet, "The Old Star Fort," *The Press and Banner* (Abbeville, SC), June 19, 1878. The elaborate celebration of 1878 was not unlike others in the Victorian era held at Cowpens, Kings Mountain and other battle sites in the region. Orations, festive music and military reviews were the order of the day during these commemorations.

76. Lyman C. Draper, *Kings Mountain and Its Heroes*, (Johnson City, TN: Overmountain Press, 1996), 498–9; Bobby Moss, *Uzal Johnson: Loyalist Surgeon*, (Blacksburg, SC: Scotia-Hibernia Press, 2000), 40–41.

77. Greene, 126; Dennis Conrad, ed., *The Papers of Nathaniel Greene* (Chapel Hill: UNC Press, 1997), 300; Joseph Johnson, *Traditions and Reminiscences of the American Revolution in the South*, (Spartanburg, SC: Reprint Co., 1972), 471–2. During the siege Cruger's wife was at the nearby Mayson plantation, three miles west of the town. Several civilians attached to the British army were at this house, unaware that the Americans had arrived and surrounded Ninety Six. Cruger's wife panicked when she received the news, and began hiding her money and valuables. Greene sent an American officer to guard the house and prevent any harm from coming to Mrs. Cruger.

78. Greene, *Historic Resource Study*, 128. This raid was launched by a group of Provincials

and Loyalist militia from the Star Fort. They destroyed the unfinished American battery before withdrawing with the captured tools and slaves. Several Virginia Continentals were killed in the raid, and the Loyalist commander Lieutenant John Roney was also killed in the firefight.

79. Ibid., 125, 129; Robert Kirkwood, *Journal and Orderly Book of Captain Robert Kirkwood*, (Wilmington, DE: Historical Society of Delaware, 1910), 18. The camp would have been laid out according to customary regulations, with guards on the perimeter, and areas established for latrines, cooking, officers' and men's tents and an artillery park. If ever discovered, the camp will be an invaluable resource, educating us about the equipment used by Greene's army in the summer of 1781 and shedding light on the life of the common soldier.

80. Stephanie Holschlag and Michael Rodeffer, *Ninety Six: Siegeworks Opposite the Star Redoubt* (National Park Service, 1976), 17; Conrad, *Papers of Nathaniel Greene*, 326. General Greene considered the lack of enough troops to do the work, and the strong defenses of the enemy, to be the two main reasons for his failure.

81. Greene, *Historic Resource Study*, 135. As armies moved across South Carolina in 1780 and 1781, they disrupted the lives of civilians. People fled their homes, refugees crowded into forts or towns, slaves ran away from masters, armed bands roamed the countryside, and law and order broke down. Perhaps these girls ran away or were kidnapped— either way they were caught up in the great migration of people in the summer of 1781.

82. Holschlag and Rodeffer, *Siegeworks*, 18; William Vaughn, Federal Pension Application. Vaughn may have been with a group that arrived after the siege had started. His recollection of "fifteen days and nights" agrees with General Greene's observations that the men often worked every other day, and sometimes every day, with few breaks.

83. Greene, *Historic Resource Study*, 149; Thomas Young, *Memoir of Major Thomas Young* (*Orion Magazine*, Nov. 1843). This tactic had worked successfully at other sites, like the siege of Fort Augusta. Thomas Young, a South Carolina militiaman, wrote that the tower was not used for very long. While the green logs were resistant to hot shot from the Loyalist cannons, it offered little protection to the soldiers manning the tower. Casualties were inflicted and the Americans abandoned it before too long.

84. Conrad, *Papers of Nathaniel Greene*, 354. Siege operations required planning, coordination, supplies and material, and organized work gangs. Interruptions could disrupt and delay important parts of the work. General Washington would have to issue similar orders during the siege of Yorktown, Virginia, just a few months later.

85. Prentice, *Archaeological Excavations*, 81; David Ek, *Mapping of the Kosciusko Tunnel (Mine)*, (Atlanta, GA: National Park Service), 2004, 1. The mine was a popular attraction long after the Revolution. Local people explored it and even added brick to support the walls. The tunnel is unstable, and has collapsed in one location. The mine tunnel ran straight toward the Star Fort, then forked into two chambers. The right-hand tunnel is

farther than the left one, being nearly twice as long and reaching almost to the fort.

86. Ibid., 138. This is another tactic that had worked at reducing other fortified sites, like Rocky Mount (although a rainstorm put out the fire), and would be used again in a few months at Fort Motte, where a British garrison would be forced to surrender.

87. Greene, *Historic Resource Study*, 143.

88. Conrad, *Papers of Nathaniel Greene*, 354; Holschlag and Rodeffer, *Siegeworks*, 65; Robert E. Lee, ed, *The Revolutionary War Memoirs of General Henry Lee*, (New York: Da Capo Press, 1998), 375.

89. Conrad, *Papers of Nathaniel Greene*, 421; Greene, *Historic Resource Study*, 162–3. It is difficult to determine losses on the day of the assault, as sources disagree. Greene wrote of the attacks on the Star Fort and stockade fort stating, "In both attacks we had upwards of 40 Men killed and Wounded, the loss was principally at the Star fort and In the Enemys ditch, the other Parties being all under cover."

90. Greene, *Historic Resource Study*, 104, 160–1; Robert D. Bass, *Ninety Six* (Lexington, SC: Sandlapper, 1977), 402; Holschlag and Rodeffer, *Siegeworks*, 79; Conrad, *Papers of Nathaniel Greene*, 421.

91. Roderick MacKenzie Strictures on Lt. Col. Tarleton's "History of the Campaigns of 1780-81, in the Southern Provinces of North America." (London: Printed for the author, 1787), 146–60.

92. Greene, *Historic Resource Study*, 161.

93. Prentice, *Archaeological Excavations*, 80–81. The cemetery appears on an 1853 map. In the 1970s the site had been covered with periwinkles, commonly found in family cemeteries in the area. The cemetery had a low earthen embankment that enclosed it, another common feature of family cemeteries. The Doziers were residents of Cambridge in the 1820s. This is an example of the layers of history at a site, for long after most of the forts and trenches were gone, people farmed, lived and worked at the site.

94. Ibid., 64.

95. Ibid.

96. Bobby Moss, *The Loyalists in the Siege of Fort Ninety Six* (Blacksburg, SC: Scotia Hibernia Press), 1999, x; Mackenzie, 146–60; Alice Waring, *The Fighting Elder* (Columbia: University of South Carolina Press, 1962), 86.

97. Prentice, *Archaeological Excavations*, 65. In 1970 archaeologists discovered the communications trench and followed it by opening sections at regular intervals. The trench was denoted by a discolored soil stain running from the Star Fort to the town. A cross section was opened in one area to reveal its depth.

98. Marjoire, Young, et. al., *South Carolina Women Patriots of the American Revolution* (1979); Lee, *Memoirs of General Henry Lee*, 374; Greene, *Historic Resource Study*, 155–6; Waring, *Fighting Elder*, 84. Lee, in his memoirs, states that the messenger was a local man who had frequently been delivering supplies to the American camp, and thus aroused no

suspicion when he drove through on this day. The legend further states that Kate Fowler had an affair with an officer in Cruger's garrison, and he left her at the end of the war. Another legend states that Kate Fowler received the message and arranged to have a man deliver it to the fort.

Many women did serve as messengers and acted as spies for both sides during the conflict, including several well-known ladies from South Carolina. Whether it was a man or woman who delivered the message, the important thing was that Cruger now knew he could reject any surrender terms and hold out for Rawdon to reach him. Whatever Kate Fowler's true identity and role was, local legends affirm that she was somehow involved with getting the news to Cruger.

99. Greene, *Historic Resource Study,* 55; Prentice, *Archaeological Excavations,* 66. One site located by archaeologists in the village was a blacksmith shop, along the Charleston Road. Slag and clinkers, waste products from blacksmithing, were found here. The site is southeast of the jail. Among residents of the town were Robert Gouedy, John Savage, William Moore and William Hagood. The exact layout of lots and location of all houses has not yet been identified. In the village area several possible cellars and trash pits have been located, one of which had a bayonet.

100. Michael Roedeffer, *Ninety Six National Historic Site: Archaeological Testing of Selected Magnetic and Airphoto Anomalies* (Greenwood, SC: Backcountry Archaeology Series, 1985), 30–31.

101. Ibid., 31. Remember that you would not have seen neat grassy fields and green trees surrounding the town in 1781. With all the activity (digging trenches, cutting wood for fuel and defensive material, troops drilling in the fields), the scene would have had a more denuded and barren appearance.

102. Prentice, *Archaeological Excavations,* 67; John H. Cruger to Lord Rawdon, June 3, 1781. Cruger wrote that one hundred "old and helpless with their families" had crowded into the fort, an additional strain on supplies.

103. Moss, *Loyalists in the Siege,* 89, 59, 93; Audit Office, American Loyalist Claims, American Series 12, Number 47, Pages 363–70. *Isaac Stewart, South Carolina, Memorial.* Public Records Office, Kew, Surry, England. The research by done Dr. Moss reveals the variety of people, civilian and military, who were caught up in the siege. Captain Isaac Stewart, a local potter, lost his crops of corn, wheat and oats, and indicated in his claim for losses that, "His Houses were burnt by the Rebels at the siege of Ninety Six when al his Furniture was consumed."

104. Eric K. Williams, interview, August 20, 2005; Lorena Walsh, *From Calabar to Carter's Grove,* (Charlottesville: University of Virginia Press, 1997), 74, 197, 200; Ywone Edwards-Ingram, "An Introduction to the Archaeology of African Americans in Colonial Virginia," *Enslaving Virginia,* (Williamsburg, VA: Colonial Williamsburg Foundation, 1998), 238–54. The presence of a shell at Ninety Six, which came from the coast, raises many questions. Shells were used as currency and for jewelry by West

Africans and have been found at other eighteenth-century archaeological sites. Such an artifact, if it is indeed left from an early African American at Ninety Six, is an important clue in how Africans retained aspects of their culture in English colonial society.

105. Stephanie Holschlag, Michael Rodeffer, and Marvin Cann. *Ninety Six: The Jail.* (National Park Service, 1976), 60, 66. An estimated forty-three thousand bricks were needed to build this formidable structure. The jail was probably the most impressive building at Ninety Six, giving this frontier town a semblance of permanence. The foundation walls were found by archaeologists to be two and a half feet thick.

106. Moss, *Loyalists in the Siege,* 138; Greene, *Historic Resource Study,* 48. There were many men from both armies who had at one time or other been a prisoner in the Ninety Six gaol. As either force held the town over the course of the war, the jail was used to hold prisoners of the other side.

107. Holschlag, Rodeffer, and Cann, *Ninety Six: The Jail,* 25.

108. Greene, *Historic Resource Study,* 150; Moss, *Loyalists in the Siege* 27, 39; Thomas Young; Waring, *Fighting Elder,* 85; Wilson and Bennet. One local tradition tells of Loyalist soldiers disguising themselves as women to retrieve water. The Americans would fire on anyone but women who approached. The Americans then found that Cruger's men were coming disguised as women, and then fired on anyone who approached the stream. This story seems to originate in an 1878 newspaper article. Unfortunately there is not more information on this issue, and the story cannot be traced back to contemporary sources.

   Thomas Young wrote that,

As we every day got our parallels nearer the garrison, we could see them very plain when they went out to a brook or spring for water. The Americans had constructed a sort of moving battery, but as the cannon of the fort were brought to bear upon it, they were forced to abandon the use of it. It had not been used for some time, when an idea struck old Squire Kennedy (who was an excellent marksman) that he could pick off a man now and then as they went to the spring. He and I took our rifles and went into the woods to practice at 200 yards. We were arrested and taken before an officer, to whom we gave excuse and design. He laughed, and told us to practice no more, but to try our luck from the battery if we wanted to, so we took our position, and as a fellow came down to the spring, Kennedy fired and he fell; several ran out and gathered round him, and among them I noticed one man raise his head, and look round as if he wondered where that shot could have come from I touched my trigger and he fell, and we made off, for fear it might be our time to fall next.

109. Prentice, *Archaeological Excavations,* 71.

110. Ibid.; Stephanie Holschlag and Michael Rodeffer, *Ninety Six: The stockade fort on the Right,* (National Park Service, 1976), 18.

111. Conrad, *Papers of Nathaniel Greene,* 354; Christopher Ward, *The Delaware Continentals,* (Wilmington, DE: Historical Society of Delaware, 1941), 447, 451; Greene, *Historic Resource Study,* 147; William Seymour, *A Journal of the Southern Expedition, 1780–83*

(*Pennsylvania Magazine of History and Biography*, VII, 1883: 286–98, 377–94), 383. When Lee and Pickens arrived from capturing Augusta, Greene had them start to besiege the stockade fort. They were joined by the Delaware Regiment, one of Greene's best and most experienced units. The American army was encouraged by the news of Augusta's capture and the arrival of these much needed reinforcements.

112. Lee, *Memoirs of General Henry Lee*, 373–4; Greene, *Historic Resource Study*, 147–8; Edward Sims, Federal Pension Application. Sims, who enlisted in 1780 with the Maryland Line, transferred to the Legion light infantry. He served at Cowpens and was in the party that made the attack on the stockade fort. He recalled the incident clearly and indicated his inability to work in his pension application over fifty years later. Lee wrote that the men who made the effort had to crawl forward on the ground and made it to the ditch surrounding the fort before being discovered.

113. Ward, *The Delaware Continentals*, 451. Robert Kirkwood, commander of the Delaware Regiment, wrote that the stockade fort held out "about an hour" before it fell. While often overlooked, fierce fighting raged in and around the stockade fort as the Americans attacked and took this position, then began exchanging fire with the town across the valley.

114. Prentice, *Archaeological Excavations*, 61.

115. Conrad, *Papers of Nathaniel Greene*, 363.

116. Greene, *Historic Resource Study*, 167–8; Robert Ellis, Federal Pension Application, S26084; Lyman C. Draper, *Sumter Papers*, 11VV537. Captain Joseph Pickens, brother of General Andrew Pickens, was apparently shot early in the siege, recognized by a Loyalist neighbor inside the defenses. This is a prime example of the bitterness that divided the settlers of the region during the conflict. Andrew was apparently not yet at Ninety Six; he was still besieging Augusta.

117. Greene, *Historic Resource Study*, 167; Ward, *The Delaware Continentals*, 452. These figures are based on the army's official returns.

118. Bass, *Ninety Six*, 406. There is no record of where the dead of either side were buried. Greene's army would have had to establish a camp cemetery during the siege operation, and Cruger's forces would have had to deal with their casualties in their confined space. After the attack, when the truce was established, the Americans may have buried their dead in the trenches in front of the Star Fort. Hopefully future archaeology will resolve this issue.

119. Bass, *Ninety Six*, 409–12; Greene, *Historic Resource Study*, 169, 172; Ward, *Delaware Continentals* 452; Moss, 121; AO 12/49/389-93; 3 DD346. Rawdon's force included detachments from the Third, Nineteenth, and Thirtieth Regiments, newly arrived from Ireland and not acclimated to the intense heat, as well as men from the Sixty-fourth, Seventh and Eighty-fourth. They were joined by Loyalist troops from the Jackson Creek and Spartan Militia Regiments and Orangeburg Light Dragoons.

Some South Carolina Loyalists, like David Bleakney, had to leave his family behind until they could join him later. The retreat was a bitter disappointment for the Americans; militiaman Patrick Cain recalled that they had "vigorously prosecuted" the siege to no avail.

120. Margaret Watson and Louise Watson, *Tombstone Inscriptions from Family Graveyards in Greenwood County*, (Greenwood, SC: Drinkard Printing Co., 1972), 39.

121. Gibbes, 221. The first battle of Ninety Six has been largely neglected by historians, and receives less attention at the park than the 1781 siege. The 1775 battle set the stage for years to come, assuring American control of the Backcountry and forcing Loyalists to lay low and wait for an opportunity for revenge.

122. Ibid., 215; Greene, *Historic Resource Study*, 69.

123. Moss, x. The core of this army—the Maryland, Delaware, and Virginia Continentals—fought at Guilford Courthouse together, and would do so again in three months at Eutaw Springs.

124. Moss; Greene, *Historic Resource Study*, 113. Dr. Moss insists that he did not find all of the Loyalists present, indicating that there were well over twelve hundred soldiers, in addition to civilians. Keeping such a large force supplied with food and water would have been a real challenge for Cruger.

125. Ibid.

126. Ibid. While the American victory at Kings Mountain was important and did eliminate Ferguson's army, the loss of Loyalist troops was actually short-lived. Most of the prisoners taken that day escaped, many fleeing to Ninety Six. While many had had enough of military service after Kings Mountain, some did manage to rejoin the British and fight again.

127. Joseph Kaufmann, "Medieval Sieges to Vaban," Presentation at the Yorktown Symposium, Yorktown, Virginia, November 12, 2004.

128. Ibid.

129. Ibid.

130. Conrad, *Papers of Nathaniel Greene*, 326, 363.

131. Greene, *Historic Resource Study*, 191.

132. Ibid.

133. Ibid., 48; Brown, *South Carolina Regulators*, 132. About thirty-five in 1768, Mayson would be one of the most influential people at Ninety Six. He served as justice of the peace and militia officer, was a Regulator leader, and during the Revolution served in the state's provisional congress and as a militia officer. Afterward he continued as a community leader and helped found Cambridge.

Bibliography

Audit Office, American Loyalist Claims, American Series 12, Number 49, Pages 389–393. "David Bleakney, South Carolina, Memorial." Public Records Office, Kew, Surry, England.

———. American Series 12, Number 50, Pages 86–92. "Richard King, South Carolina, Memorial." Public Records Office, Kew, Surry, England.

———. American Series 12, Number 47, Pages 363–70. "Isaac Stewart, South Carolina, Memorial." Public Records Office, Kew, Surry, England.

Bass, Robert D. *Ninety Six*. Lexington, SC: Sandlapper Press, 1977.

Brown, Richard M. *The South Carolina Regulators*. Cambridge, MA: Belknap Press, 1963.

Conrad, Dennis, ed. *The Papers of Nathaniel Greene*. Chapel Hill: University North Carolina Press, 1997.

Draper, Lyman C. *Kings Mountain and Its Heroes*. Johnson City, TN: Overmountain Press, 1996.

———. Thomas Sumter Papers, Draper Manuscript Collection. Madison: State Historical Society of Wisconsin (DD Series).

Dunkerly, Robert M. *More Than Roman Valor*. Baltimore: PublishAmerica, 2003.

Edwards-Ingram, Ywone. "An Introduction to the Archaeology of African Americans in Colonial Virginia." In *Enslaving Virginia*. Williamsburg: Colonial Williamsburg Foundation, 1998, 238–47.

Ek, David. *Mapping of the Kosciusko Tunnel (Mine)*. Atlanta, GA: National Park Service, 2004.

Gibbes, R.W. *Documentary History of the American Revolution*. Vol. 1. Spartanburg, SC: Reprint Co., 1972.

Greene, Jerome. *Historic Resource Study and Historic Structure Report, Ninety Six: A Historical Narrative*. Denver: National Park Service, 1978.

Holschlag, Stephanie, and Michael Rodeffer. *Ninety Six: Siegeworks Opposite the Star Redoubt*. National Park Service, 1976.

————. *Ninety Six: Exploratory Excavations in the Village*. National Park Service, 1977.

————. *Ninety Six: The Stockade Fort on the Right*. National Park Service, 1976.

Holschlag, Stephanie, Michael Rodeffer and Marvin Cann. *Ninety Six: The Jail*. National Park Service, 1976.

Holschlag, Stephanie, Michael Rodeffer and Mary Cann. *Greenwood County: An Archaeological Survey*. Greenwood, SC: Lander College, 1979.

Johnson, Joseph. *Traditions and Reminiscences of the American Revolution in the South*. Spartanburg, SC: Reprint Co., 1972.

Kaufmann, Joseph. "Medieval Sieges to Vaban," Presentation at the Yorktown Symposium, Yorktown, VA, November 12, 2004

Kirkwood, Robert. *Journal and Order Book of Captain Robert Kirkwood*. Wilmington: Historical Society of Delaware, 1910.

Lee, Robert E., ed. *The Revolutionary War Memoirs of General Henry Lee*. New York: Da Capo Press, 1998.

Mackenzie, Roderick. *Strictures on Lt. Col. Tarleton's "History of the Campaigns of 1780–81, in the Southern Provinces of North America."* London: Printed for the author, 1787.

Bibliography

McDowell, William. *The Colonial Records of South Carolina. Documents Relating to Indian Affairs.* Columbia: South Carolina Archives Department, 1958.

Moss, Bobby. *The Loyalists in the Siege of Fort Ninety Six.* Blacksburg, SC: Scotia Hibernia Press, 1999.

———. *Uzal Johnson: Loyalist Surgeon.* Blacksburg, SC: Scotia Hibernia Press, 2000.

Nelson, Paul. *General James Grant.* Gainesville: University of Florida Press, 1993.

Pope, Thomas H. *The History of Newberry County.* Columbia: University of South Carolina Press, 1973.

Prentice, Guy. *Archaeological Excavations Conducted at Ninety Six National Historic Site.* Tallahassee, FL: Southeast Archaeological Center, 2002.

Robinson, W. Stitt. *James Glen.* Westport, CT: Greenwood Press, 1966.

Rodeffer, Michael. *Ninety Six National Historic Site: Archaeological Testing of Selected Magnetic and Airphoto Anomalies.* Greenwood, SC: Backcountry Archaeology Series, 1985.

Seymour, William. *A Journal of the Southern Expedition, 1780–83.* Pennsylvania Magazine of History and Biography, Vol. VII (1881): 286–98, 377–94.

Sims, Edward. Federal Pension Application. S46524. Revolutionary War Pension Applications and Bounty-Land Warrant Application Files, National Archives, Washington, D.C.

Vaughn, William. Federal Pension Application. W2708. Revolutionary War Pension Applications and Bounty-Land Warrant Application Files, National Archives, Washington, D.C.

Walsh, Lorena. *From Calabar to Carter's Grove.* Charlottesville: University of Virginia Press, 1997.

Ward, Christopher. *The Delaware Continentals.* Wilmington: Historical Society of Delaware, 1941.

Waring, Alice. *The Fighting Elder.* Columbia: University of South Carolina Press, 1962.

Watson, Margaret. *Greenwood County Sketches*. Greenwood, SC: Attic Press Inc., 1970.

Watson, Margaret and Louise Watson. *Tombstone Inscriptions from Family Graveyards in Greenwood County*. Greenwood, SC: Drinkard Printing Co., 1972.

Wilson, Hugh, and W.C. Bennet. "The Old Star Fort." *Press and Banner*, Abbeville, SC, June 19, 1878.

Young, Marjoire, et al. *South Carolina Women Patriots of the American Revolution*. 1979.

Young, Thomas. "Memoir of Major Thomas Young." *Orion Magazine*, November 1843.

Index

W

About the Authors

Robert M. Dunkerly is currently a park ranger at Kings Mountain National Military Park, where he is a historic weapons safety officer. He has worked at several other historic sites, including Gettysburg, Stones River, Jamestown, Washington's Birthplace, Bushy Run and Colonial Williamsburg. He has also worked as an archaeologist in the Williamsburg, Virginia, area.

Eric K. Williams serves as the chief park ranger and historian at Ninety Six National Historic Site. He is also a historic weapons safety officer, and wrote the National Park Service manual for swivel gun demonstrations. Eric is a life member of the Sons of the American Revolution and is an eighteenth-century reenactor, portraying an apothecary.